Perspectives on Modern World History

Japan's 2011 Natural Disasters and Nuclear Meltdown

1st EDITION

Perspectives on Modern World History

Japan's 2011 Natural Disasters and Nuclear Meltdown

Myra Immell

Editor

GREENHAVEN PRESS
A part of Gale, Cengage Learning

GALE
CENGAGE Learning®

Farmington Hills, Mich • San Francisco • New York • Waterville, Maine
Meriden. Conn • Mason. Ohio • Chicago

GALE
CENGAGE Learning·

Elizabeth Des Chenes, *Director, Content Strategy*
Cynthia Sanner, *Publisher*
Douglas Dentino, *Manager, New Product*

© 2014 Greenhaven Press, a part of Gale, Cengage Learning.

WCN: 01-100-101

For more information, contact:
Greenhaven Press
27500 Drake Rd.
Farmington Hills, MI 48331-3535
Or you can visit our Internet site at gale.cengage.com.

For product information and technology assistance, contact us at
Gale Customer Support, 1-800-877-4253.

For permission to use material from this text or product, submit all requests online at
www.cengage.com/permissions.

Further permissions questions can be e-mailed to permissionrequest@cengage.com.

Articles in Greenhaven Press anthologies are often edited for length to meet page requirements. In addition, original titles of these works are changed to clearly present the main thesis and to explicitly indicate the author's opinion. Every effort is made to ensure that Greenhaven Press accurately reflects the original intent of the authors. Every effort has been made to trace the owners of copyrighted material.

Cover images © Pallava Bagla/Corbis, and © yankane/Shutterstock.com.

LIBRARY OF CONGRESS CATALOGING-IN-PUBLICATION DATA

Japan's 2011 natural disasters and nuclear meltdown / Myra Immell, book editor.
    pages cm. -- (Perspectives on modern world history)
    Summary: "Perspectives on Modern World History: Japan's 2011 Natural Disasters and Nuclear Meltdown: The series provides basic historical information on a significant event in modern world history, presents the controversies surrounding the event, and provides first-person narratives"-- Provided by publisher.
    Includes bibliographical references and index.
    ISBN 978-0-7377-6973-9 (hardback)
    1. Tohoku Earthquake and Tsunami, Japan, 2011. 2. Fukushima Nuclear Disaster, Japan, 2011. I. Immell, Myra.
    HV6002011.T64 J37 2014
    952.05'12--dc23
                                                                        2013035654

Printed in the United States of America
1 2 3 4 5 6 7 18 17 16 15 14

CONTENTS

A journalist for an international news organization reports on a second explosion at Japan's Fukushima Daiichi nuclear power plant, which was already suffering damage from the March 2011 earthquake and tsunami, and on the potential risk of a major radioactive leak.

A former tsunami researcher in Japan contends that Japan was well prepared for disaster. The area where disaster struck represents state-of-the-art readiness for earthquake and tsunami disasters.

nuclear meltdown and analyzes the possibility that the crises created by those disasters will stimulate Japan to renew itself.

CHAPTER 3

Personal Narratives

bus drive to his destination. He talks about the radiation readings he monitored along the way and shares what he witnessed inside the plant.

Marcus Erikson

A US scientist recounts his experience during a June 2012 expedition to hunt down the tons of material washed into the ocean by the 2011 tsunami. He describes the journey, how he and the other team members felt, and what they found.

FOREWORD

"History cannot give us a program for the future, but it can give us a fuller understanding of ourselves, and of our common humanity, so that we can better face the future."
—Robert Penn Warren,
American poet and novelist

The history of each nation is punctuated by momentous events that represent turning points for that nation, with an impact felt far beyond its borders. These events—displaying the full range of human capabilities, from violence, greed, and ignorance to heroism, courage, and strength—are nearly always complicated and multifaceted. Any student of history faces the challenge of grasping the many strands that constitute such world-changing events as wars, social movements, and environmental disasters. But understanding these significant historic events can be enhanced by exposure to a variety of perspectives, whether of people involved intimately or of ones observing from a distance of miles or years. Understanding can also be increased by learning about the controversies surrounding such events and exploring hot-button issues from multiple angles. Finally, true understanding of important historic events involves knowledge of the events' human impact—of the ways such events affected people in their everyday lives—all over the world.

Perspectives on Modern World History examines global historic events from the twentieth century onward by presenting analysis and observation from numerous vantage points. Each volume offers high school, early college level, and general interest readers a thematically arranged anthology of previously published materials that address a major historical event, with an emphasis on international coverage. Each volume opens with background information on the event, then presents the controversies surrounding that event, and concludes with first-person narratives from people who lived through the event or were affected by it. By providing primary sources from the time of the event, as well as relevant commentary surrounding the event, this series can be used to inform debate, help develop critical thinking skills, increase global awareness, and enhance an understanding of international perspectives on history.

Material in each volume is selected from a diverse range of sources, including journals, magazines, newspapers, nonfiction books, personal narratives, speeches, congressional testimony, government documents, pamphlets, organization newsletters, and position papers. Articles taken from these sources are carefully edited and introduced to provide context and background. Each volume of Perspectives on Modern World History includes an array of views on events of global significance. Much of the material comes from international sources and from US sources that provide extensive international coverage.

Each volume in the Perspectives on Modern World History series also includes:

- A full-color **world map**, offering context and geographic perspective.
- An annotated **table of contents** that provides a brief summary of each essay in the volume.
- An **introduction** specific to the volume topic.
- For each viewpoint, a brief **introduction** that has notes about the author and source of the viewpoint, and that provides a summary of its main points.
- Full-color **charts**, **graphs**, **maps**, and other visual representations.

- Informational **sidebars** that explore the lives of key individuals, give background on historical events, or explain scientific or technical concepts.
- A **glossary** that defines key terms, as needed.
- A **chronology** of important dates preceding, during, and immediately following the event.
- A **bibliography** of additional books, periodicals, and websites for further research.
- A comprehensive **subject index** that offers access to people, places, and events cited in the text.

Perspectives on Modern World History is designed for a broad spectrum of readers who want to learn more about not only history but also current events, political science, government, international relations, and sociology—students doing research for class assignments or debates, teachers and faculty seeking to supplement course materials, and others wanting to improve their understanding of history. Each volume of Perspectives on Modern World History is designed to illuminate a complicated event, to spark debate, and to show the human perspective behind the world's most significant happenings of recent decades.

INTRODUCTION

On March 16, 2011, as Japan was reeling from an earthquake, a tsunami, and a nuclear emergency, NKH, Japan's national broadcaster, aired a five-minute speech addressed to the people of Japan. The speaker was Akihito, the seventy-seven-year-old emperor of Japan, and it was his very first televised speech. He spoke about the disaster relief efforts being made, the calmness and courageousness of the survivors, and hope.

During the speech, the emperor expressed his deep concern for the growing nuclear crisis. He was referring to the accident at the Fukushima Daiichi nuclear power plant located 155 miles from Tokyo, the nation's capital. "No one," he said, "can predict what will happen next." "It is," he continued, "my deepest hope that, by the effort of all those people concerned, the situation can be prevented from getting worse."

The emperor was right to be concerned. The cooling systems of the plant's nuclear reactors had been damaged by the earthquake and tsunami. Unfortunately, all efforts to control the reactors were not enough, and the situation did get worse. Two days after the emperor's speech, the Japanese government's nuclear safety agency raised the Fukushima crisis level from 4 to 5 on the international 0–7 scale of gravity for atomic accidents. About a week later, the agency again raised the level—this time to a 6. On April 11 the agency updated the level for the final time to the very top of the scale—7. Japan was now experiencing what the International Atomic Energy Agency classified as a "major accident: A major release of radioactive material with widespread health and environmental effects requiring implementation of planned and extended countermeasures." To this point in time, the only 7-rated nuclear accident ever was the 1986 Chernobyl disaster in what is now Ukraine.

As the level of Japan's crisis had grown, so had international concern. As the potential for nuclear meltdown increased, the scope of the disaster changed. It ceased to be just Japan's problem. Fallout from a nuclear meltdown could endanger many other global areas. International media began to broadcast this fear. Before long the actual facts of a nuclear meltdown got caught up in a sea of misinformation and myth. Many governments and their populations began to monitor wind currents from Japan and broadcast global radiation readings. Many expressed concern about the age of their country's nuclear plants. They began to question whether or not the necessary safeguards had been put in place and the age at which nuclear plants would no longer work the way they should. Some commentators went so far as to predict that the Fukushima meltdown would put an end to the nuclear industry.

As the public concern grew, so did that of many governments. Countries with nuclear power plants found themselves in the middle of a heated debate over nuclear energy. Discussion about how much nuclear energy, if any at all, was safe, was sparked off across the globe. Fukushima played a role in the decision by Switzerland to phase out nuclear power by 2034. It also influenced the vote in Italy to renew nuclear power, with more than 94 percent of the people voting against renewal.

Adding fuel to the growing debate over nuclear power was the May 2011 declaration by then Japanese prime minister Naoto Kan that Japan would abandon plans to build new nuclear reactors. His country, he said, needed to create a new energy policy, a policy that "should include greater reliance on renewable energy and conservation." This was a stunning departure for Japan, where nuclear energy had been a national strategic priority for decades. A year later, in May of 2012,

Japan's nuclear reactors shut down for the first time in more than forty years. Japan was nuclear free.

On September 14, 2012, the Japanese government announced a new energy policy, the "Innovative Energy and Environment Strategy." The government's intention was to "mobilize every policy resource available to achieve the abolition of nuclear power plants in the 2030s." To make this happen, the government would limit the nation's existing nuclear reactors to a forty-year life span and would not build any new ones. Most Japanese—two-thirds according to a January 2012 *Washington Post* article—favored the policy. Others, however, did not. This included major business leaders and both Western and local Japanese governments hosting nuclear sites. As a result, the Cabinet, which had to approve the entire policy for it to be binding, did not do so. Instead, it issued the following statement: "The government will promote energy and environment policy under constant examination and review, in dialogue with affected local governments and the global community, as well as seeking understanding from the general public." This left the door open to more debate—and to more change in the government response to the nuclear issue.

In December of 2012, a new prime minister, Shinzo Abe, was elected in Japan. The month before, Abe had promised that if his political party won the December elections in the Lower House of Parliament he would restart the nation's reactors. Not long after taking office, he stated that he expected there to be new construction of nuclear power plants. In a January 4, 2013, press conference, Abe responded to a reporter's question about the government stand on nuclear power:

> We will first of all determine whether or not to restart nuclear power plants on the basis of scientific safety standards. Then over the course of roughly three years we will assess the futures of existing nuclear power

plants and transition to a new stable energy mix over ten years. The new construction or replacement of nuclear power plants is not a matter that is able to be determined immediately. Naturally this is an area in which we should make our determination in accordance with the principle of gradually decreasing our degree of reliance on nuclear power to the greatest extent possible.

Abe went on to express his desire to take time to examine the situation as the government looked ahead "critically regarding the verification of the nuclear power plant accident and trends in the progress of safety technology."

A little more than a month later, in a policy speech to Japan's legislature, the National Diet, Abe once again addressed the energy issue in general and the nuclear situation in particular:

> We will formulate a responsible energy policy aimed at ensuring a stable supply of energy and lower energy costs.
>
> Reflecting on the accident at Tokyo Electric Power Company's Fukushima Daiichi Nuclear Power Station, under the Nuclear Regulation Authority, we will foster a new culture of safety that will uncompromisingly enhance the degree of safety. After doing so we will restart nuclear power plants where safety has been confirmed.
>
> We will promote the introduction of energy conservation and renewable energies to the greatest possible extent to reduce our degree of dependency on nuclear power as much as possible. At the same time, we will begin a fundamental reform of the electric system.

In late July 2013, Abe's political party, the Liberal Democratic Party, won a landslide victory in parliamentary elections. Even though polls showed that most of the Japanese people still were against nuclear energy, the government has continued to consider it a critical part of the Japanese energy mix. Abe has made it clear that he believes that Japan needs nuclear power to ensure its energy.

The 2011 triple disaster greatly changed the world-wide discussion about the safety of nuclear energy. In addition, the natural disasters influenced how many nations view disaster preparedness. *Perspectives in Modern World History: Japan's 2011 Natural Disasters and Nuclear Meltdown* provides background on the natural disasters and nuclear meltdown and details their impact on the world today.

World Map

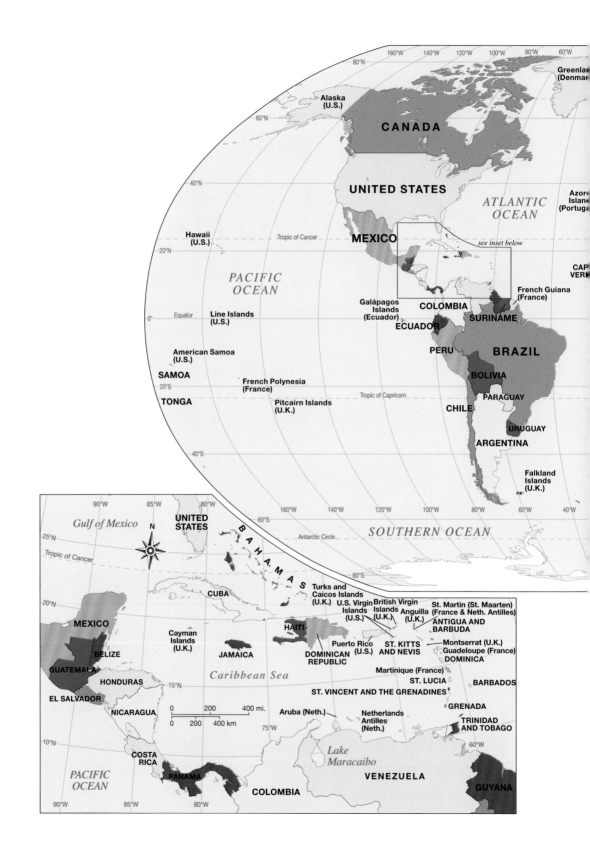

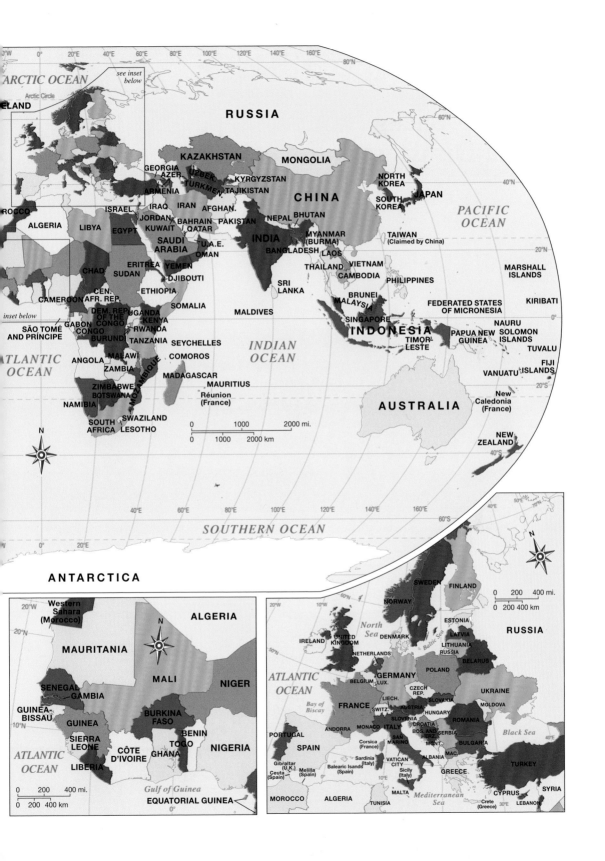

CHAPTER 1

Historical Background on Japan's 2011 Natural Disasters and Nuclear Meltdown

The 2011 Japanese Disasters: An Overview

Historic World Events

The following viewpoint provides an overview of the natural disasters and nuclear meltdown that struck Japan in March 2011. The devastation caused by these disasters was widespread, and the death toll was in the tens of thousands. The earthquake, the fifth most powerful in the past one hundred years, was the start of a powerful chain reaction. The earthquake triggered a tsunami that gobbled up everything in its path. While the nation was struggling to deal with the damage from the earthquake and tsunami, the events set off a powerful explosion that rocked the Fukushima Daiichi nuclear power plant, causing a leak in one of the plant's reactors. There was increased fear of a nuclear meltdown. Efforts to control the contamination crisis at the plant were hindered when high radiation levels were detected in the facility. Japan's stability has been severely threatened by the chain of disastrous events.

Photo on previous page: Tsunami waves rush towards ground-level oil tanks at the Fukushima Daiichi nuclear power plant on March 11, 2011. The waves destroyed critical backup generators, causing a nuclear meltdown. (© **Tokyo Electric Power Co./AP Images.**)

SOURCE. "Earthquake Hits Japan and Compromises Nuclear Power Facility, March 11 and March 12, 2011," *Historic World Events*. Farmington Hills, MI: Gale, 2011. *World History in Context.* Copyright © 2011 Cengage Learning. Reproduced by permission.

The scene is, unfortunately, all too familiar. The ground begins to shake as frightened people run for cover, and sturdy, well-built buildings sway like leaves in the wind. That was the scene in northeast Japan on March 11, 2011, at 2:46 P.M. as a magnitude 9.0 earthquake struck the island nation; in its aftermath, a 33-foot (10 meter) high wall of water generated by the quake hurtled through ill-fated towns, leaving behind indescribable devastation. The wall of water or tsunami, which means "harbor wave" in Japanese, sped inland, grabbing hold of trucks, cars, and homes—literally, anything in its path.

Japan is, of course, not the only Asian country to suffer from earthquakes and tsunamis. Nearly every year, at least one devastating tsunami strikes somewhere in the Pacific. Because they often occur in remote countries, the media gives them little coverage, leading to the mistaken belief that tsunamis are usually harmless, and rare. . . .

The earthquake that hit Japan on that Friday of March 11 was the fifth most powerful in the past century. The frantic search for survivors began immediately and continued with tens of thousands of soldiers, supported by ships and helicopters, deployed on rescue and relief missions. The United Nations coordinated international disaster relief operations, with President Barack Obama promising U.S. assistance. Japan's Kyodo news agency reported that about 300,000 people were evacuated from their homes nationwide, most huddling together in temporary shelters in near-freezing temperatures. Five-and-a-half million people were without power, while 3,400 buildings had either been destroyed or damaged. Four trains were unaccounted for after the tsunami. In hardest-hit Sendai, 180 miles (300 kilometers) northeast of Tokyo, rescue workers searched through the rubble looking for survivors. Buildings, cars, boats, trains, and small planes could be seen in aerial footage, strewn like toys over the landscape of the devastated town. Huge shipping containers had been carried away from the harbor and smashed into buildings with great force. Police reported that between 200 and 300 bodies were found in just one section of Sendai alone. "The tsunami was unbelievably fast," said a stunned Koichi Takairin, a 34-year-old truck driver who witnessed the giant wave hit Sendai from inside his four-ton rig. "Smaller cars were being swept around me. All I could do was sit in my truck." Much of the town of Rikuzentakada, Iwate, was destroyed and almost completely underwater; NHK, Japan's national public broadcasting organization, reported that soldiers had found up to 400 bodies there. NHK also reported that, in the port city of Minamisanriku, about 7,500 people had been evacuated to 25 shelters, but the rest of the town's inhabitants—some 10,000 people—were missing. In the first days after the disaster, authorities estimated the death toll would exceed 1,800; sadly, by March 27, it had risen to 10,668, with 16,574 still missing.

> As a consequence of the earthquake and its accompanying tsunami, on Saturday, March 12, a powerful explosion rocked the Fukushima Daiichi nuclear power plant.

As a consequence of the earthquake and its accompanying tsunami, on Saturday, March 12, a powerful explosion rocked the Fukushima Daiichi nuclear power plant, 140 miles (220 kilometers) northeast of Tokyo, causing a leak in the facility's No. 1 reactor. The blast raised immediate fears of a nuclear meltdown at the plant; the plant's operator, the Tokyo Electric Power Company (TEPCO), prepared to release some steam to relieve pressure in the No. 3 reactor after a failure was detected in its cooling system. Authorities assured the public that, although a building housing a reactor had been destroyed, the reactor itself was intact.

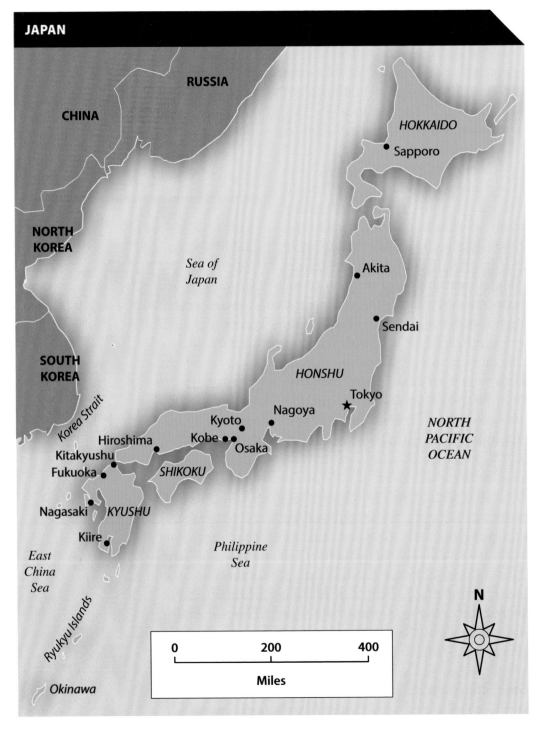

JAPAN

RUSSIA

CHINA

HOKKAIDO
● Sapporo

NORTH
KOREA

*Sea of
Japan*

● Akita

● Sendai

SOUTH
KOREA

HONSHU

Tokyo
★

Korea Strait

Kyoto
Kobe ● ●
● Nagoya

Hiroshima
Kitakyushu ●
Fukuoka ●

Osaka

SHIKOKU

*NORTH
PACIFIC
OCEAN*

Nagasaki ●
Kiire ●

KYUSHU

*East
China
Sea*

*Philippine
Sea*

N

Ryukyu Islands

0   200   400

Miles

Okinawa

The incident raised the specter of a repeat of previous nuclear meltdowns, the most serious of which were the Three Mile Island accident in the United States in 1979 and the Chernobyl nuclear disaster in the Soviet Union in 1986. Before news of the problem with reactor No. 3 was announced, an official at the Japan Nuclear Energy Safety Organization—JNES—rated the incident at Fukushima a 4 according to the International Nuclear and Radiological Event Scale (INES). Three Mile Island was rated 5 while Chernobyl was rated 7 on a scale of 1 to 7. . . .

The Impact of the Nuclear Meltdown

In the aftermath of the explosion at Fukushima, the question to answer was whether the reactor was shut down before any melting occurred, which would have significantly reduced the risk of radioactive materials entering the environment. This question could not be answered quickly or easily. The detection of cesium isotopes outside the power station buildings seemed to imply that the core had been exposed to the air. Officials attempted to reassure the public, insisting that only small amounts of radiation had been expelled as part of the measures to safeguard the reactor's stability; they were nothing compared to the radioactive clouds emitted at Chernobyl twenty-five years before. According to a Japanese government spokesperson, Yukio Edano, the steel container encasing the reactor had not been ruptured, and sea water was being pumped into the site to lower temperatures. However, though Japan had developed a successful nuclear power program, there had already been some scandals associated with the industry, involving suspected falsification of nuclear plant safety records. Hasty reassurances from TEPCO were unlikely to satisfy an already skittish and frightened population, especially in light of statements made by the JNES estimating [that] the number of people exposed to radiation from the Fukushima Daiichi plant could reach one hundred and sixty.

Within 24 hours of the explosion, the evacuation zone around the damaged nuclear plant had been expanded from 10 kilometers (6.2 miles) to 20 kilometers (12.4 miles), and a state of emergency had been declared. An estimated 200,000 people were evacuated from areas near the Fukushima plant, according to the International Atomic Energy Agency, and authorities prepared to dispense iodine to people in the vicinity to protect them from radioactive exposure. Workers clad in protective gear examined people gathering at evacuation centers to detect any such exposure.

On Sunday, March 19, Japan's efforts to control the nuclear contamination crisis at the Fukushima Daiichi plant experienced a major setback when disturbingly high radiation levels were detected in a flooded area inside the facility. TEPCO admitted the radiation levels in the water were at least four times the allowable exposure levels for personnel at the plant and 100,000 times more than water normally found at a nuclear facility. The setback would likely disrupt cleanup activities for an indefinite period and make it very difficult to bring the crisis under control, as workers would only be able to stay at the cleanup site for up to 15 minutes at a time.

> The earthquake and tsunami, as well as the explosion and subsequent leak at Fukushima, pose a major challenge to Japan's stability.

The earthquake and tsunami, as well as the explosion and subsequent leak at Fukushima, pose a major challenge to Japan's stability. The disaster hit just as the world's third-largest economy began to emerge from a major economic crisis. However, many have great confidence in the Japanese people's ability to overcome adversity and to rebuild their country. John V. Roos, U.S. Ambassador to Japan, may have expressed it best when

This combination of photos shows the coast of Japan at Minamisoma before (top), during (middle), and after (bottom) the tsunami hit. (© Jiji Press/AFP/Getty Images.)

he stated on June 12, 2011, the three-month anniversary of the explosion at the power plant, ". . . the strength and the resilience and the power of the Japanese people is so inspiring to the world that there is nothing that this country cannot accomplish."

Japan Shattered; First the Quakes, Then the Tsunami—Now, the Devastation of Possible Nuclear Meltdown

Chico Harlan

In the following viewpoint, a journalist reports on the enormous toll taken on the land and people of Japan by the earthquake and tsunami that ravaged the nation's northeast coast on March 11, 2011, and on the government response to a potential nuclear crisis in Fukushima. As a result of these disasters, large numbers of people are dead or missing, and Japan's infrastructure has been seriously compromised. The Japanese prime minister pledged that the government would do everything in its power to curtail the damage. He urged the Japanese people to take action and work together to help each other and asked the international community to assist in their efforts. A multitude of countries were quick to respond to the call for assistance. Chico Harlan is a foreign correspondent for the *Washington Post.* He formerly served as a staff writer at the *Pittsburgh Post-Gazette* and the (Sydney) *Daily-Telegraph.*

A bulldozing tsunami triggered by an 8.9-magnitude earthquake devastated the northeast coast of Japan on Friday [March 11, 2011], turning cars into driftwood, washing away neighbourhoods and leaving this industrialized country bracing for an epic humanitarian disaster.

Some estimates say 1,300 people have died and news outlets reported that many of the deaths were from drowning. Thousands more people have been reported missing, and officials say they expect the death toll to climb steeply.

The government warned there could be a radiation leak from nuclear reactors in Fukushima whose cooling system was knocked out by the quake. Prime Minister Naoto Kan ordered an evacuation zone expanded to 10 kilometres from three. Thousands of people have been ordered out of the area.

"It's possible that radioactive material in the reactor vessel could leak outside, but the amount is expected to be small, and the wind blowing towards the sea will be considered," chief cabinet secretary Yukio Edano told a news conference.

As authorities battled to contain rising pressure at the Fukushima facility, 240 kilometres north of Tokyo, officials called for calm and said a meltdown remained unlikely.

This earthquake, the fifth largest worldwide since 1900 and the strongest ever to strike Japan, will redefine

Operation Tomodachi

Operation Tomodachi [Friendship] helped boost the image of US forces in Japan. Surveys found that opinion in Japan toward the United States following the operation was the most favorable in nearly a decade. From March 12 [2011] to about May 11 [2011], working under guidance from the SDF [Japan Self-Defense Force], the operation deployed 24 US naval ships, 189 aircraft, and almost 24,000 US service members. Both countries have reportedly shared the $90 million cost.

During the first week after the quake and tsunami, US forces rescued about 20,000 people and restored transportation facilities, including Sendai Airport, a virtual hub for the region. The operation was also an important asset during the early stages of the Fukushima Daiichi plant accident. The US Navy provided almost two million liters of fresh water to cool the plant's reactors, and the Marine Corps Chemical Biological Incident Response Force trained SDF troops operating nearby. US manned aerial drones flew over the plant to monitor and collect data for the Japanese government. On-the-ground assistance was provided by officials from the NRC [US Nuclear Regulatory Commission] and the US Defense and Energy Departments.

Called "the single largest humanitarian relief effort in American history," the peacetime mission has been lauded by both governments and mainstream press as a great success.

SOURCE. *Lucy Birmingham and David McNeill,* Strong in the Rain: Surviving Japan's Earthquake, Tsunami, and Fukushima Nuclear Disaster. *New York: Palgrave Macmillan, 2012, p. 133.*

the challenges facing a country already burdened by debt, economic stagnation and depopulation.

A Need for Monumental Relief Efforts

A grim accounting of lost infrastructure and lives lies ahead. But as of this morning, Japan remained a country reckoning with images, not numbers. Describing what could become one of the country's deepest traumas since the Second World War, television broadcasters appeared on camera wearing helmets as a precaution against aftershocks. People in Tokyo shared YouTube videos of downtown skyscrapers swaying back and forth and witnesses screaming.

Initial reports from the hardest-hit part of the country pointed to the monumental relief efforts ahead. Much of the northern city of Kesennuma was on fire. Japanese officials said they had lost contact with four trains. Local police reported that 200 to 300 bodies had been found in one area of Sendai, the capital of Miyagi Prefecture and the population centre closest to the quake's epicentre.

Prime Minister Naoto Kan addressed the nation, saying the government will do "everything possible to minimize the damage." He called for international assistance, and for Japanese to help one another. "We ask the people of Japan to exercise the spirit of fraternity and act fast and to assist one's family and neighbours."

Throughout the country, transportation was halted and mobile-phone networks were jammed. Tokyo's main Narita international airport halted flights for much of Friday afternoon. Stranded workers in downtown Tokyo crowded around televisions, watching the NHK network replay a loop of the images: slow-dancing Tokyo skyscrapers and building-blitzing waves. Television footage showed towering walls of water surging toward the shoreline, pulling cars into the surf and discarding ships on land.

Consumers flocked to grocery and convenience stores, clearing shelves. The government urged citizens to conserve supplies, and residents in the north reported shortages.

"It is snowing in Sendai and blankets and food are not abundant," Tamotsu Watanabe, a staff member for the Sendai city government, said this morning [March 12, 2011]. "We haven't been able to catch up with the magnitude of things."

Dozens of countries and states issued tsunami alerts—mostly in the Pacific Rim including Canada, but also in Hawaii and California. But the waves that reached Hawaii about 8 A.M. Ottawa time were relatively modest, and the tsunami had only isolated impact on the North American coast.

In Washington, U.S. President Barack Obama said he was "heartbroken" by the tragedy and offered "whatever

Sendai, the capital of the Miyagi Prefecture, was one of the hardest hit areas in the 2011 disaster. (© Foto24/ Gallo Images/Getty Images.)

assistance is needed." The U.S. military redeployed several ships toward Japan on Friday and began preparing for humanitarian relief missions in the expectation that it would be asked to help. The unfolding natural disaster prompted offers of search-and-rescue help from 50 countries, including Canada and China.

About 70 search-and-rescue teams have been put on standby around the world awaiting a Japanese government request for assistance in digging out survivors, according to Nicholas Reader, a spokesman for the UN Office for the Coordination of Humanitarian Affairs.

"Our initial assessment indicates that there has already been enormous damage," said Yukio Edano, the government's top spokesman. "We will make maximum relief effort based on that assessment."

> 'Our initial assessment indicates that there has already been enormous damage,' said Yukio Edano, the government's top spokesman.

Reacting to the Quake and Its Aftershocks

The quake struck at 2:46 P.M. local time (12:46 A.M. EST) about 140 kilometres off the coast of Miyagi Prefecture, a mostly rural but still densely populated part of Honshu, Japan's largest island.

Tokyo—about 400 kilometres south of the epicentre—appeared to escape massive damage, although some fires were reported and buildings shook violently for several minutes during the initial quake. At least two million people were without power in the capital.

Workers and residents fled from buildings and refused to return indoors, terrified by the aftershocks that continued for hours. In all, Japan felt dozens of aftershocks, some as strong as a 7.1 magnitude.

With the normally reliable mass transit system shut down, thousands of commuters from Tokyo's expansive suburbs were stranded, unable to find taxis. Shelters opened their doors to accommodate them; some spent the night in temples, university buildings and concert halls.

Japan has invested significant resources in preparing itself. A strict building code enacted in 1981 requires structures to be built using ductile reinforced concrete, which provides flexibility that can help withstand significant tremors.

The 1995 Kobe earthquake—until Friday the country's most devastating—levelled many buildings constructed before the 1981 code was in place. The death toll from that earthquake, which struck a much more heavily populated area, rose above 6,000.

Since the Kobe quake, many public buildings have been reinforced.

A Second Blast at the Fukushima Nuclear Plant

Ron Synovitz

In the following viewpoint, a journalist for an international news and broadcast organization details the situation that has led Japanese authorities to rush to prevent a nuclear meltdown at the Fukushima Daiichi plant along Japan's northeastern coast. Several hundred thousand people have been evacuated from the area around the nuclear complex from which low-level radiation has been released. The crisis at Fukushima has had a major effect on the thinking of some European Union nations about their nuclear energy policies and most likely will prompt a debate about the life span of nuclear reactors. Meanwhile millions of people living along Japan's northeastern coast have been suffering the effects of the earthquake and tsunami that struck the area. And, because of falling stock prices, the nation is suffering economically as well.

SOURCE. Ron Synovitz, "Second Blast at Japanese Nuclear Plant After Quake, Tsunami," Radio Free Europe/Radio Liberty, March 14, 2011. Copyright © 2011 by RFE/RL, Inc. Reprinted with the permission of Radio Free Europe/Radio Liberty, 1201 Connecticut Ave NW, Suite 400, Washington, DC 20036. www.rferl.org.

Ron Synovitz is a senior correspondent with Radio Free Europe/ Radio Liberty, one of the most comprehensive news operations worldwide.

Japanese authorities are racing to prevent a catastrophic meltdown at the Fukushima nuclear power plant, which was badly damaged in the March 11 [2011] earthquake and tsunami.

Officials from Tokyo Electric Power Company said the fuel rods appear to be melting inside all three of the most damaged nuclear reactors after they were exposed when a steam vent failed to open properly.

Chief Cabinet Secretary Yukio Edano said: "Although we cannot directly check it, it's highly likely happening."

It is the second time fuel rods at the reactor have become exposed. Earlier on March 14 [2011], officials frantically pumped seawater into the second reactor in an attempt to cool the rods.

If the 4-meter rods remain exposed too long, the temperatures in the core could rise to a level where they melt through the protective steel walls.

The containment vessel that encases the core is supposed to protect the outside environment from any crisis inside, but the 9-magnitude earthquake that shook the country last week may have compromised the structural integrity of the vessel.

But in a statement, the Vienna-based head of the UN [United Nations] nuclear watchdog agency, Yukiya Amano, said the reactor vessels are intact and so far the radiation release has been "limited."

"The nuclear plants have been shaken, flooded, and cut off from electricity," Amano said. "Operators have suffered personal tragedies. But the reactor vessels have held and radioactive release is limited."

Amano said Japan has officially asked it to send a team of experts to help it deal with the crisis.

Radiation Is Released

The Japanese government has told citizens that the risk of a major radioactive leak remains small. Some 200,000 people have been evacuated from a 20-kilometer radius around the plant.

Low-level radiation has already been released by explosions on March 12 [2011] and early on March 14 [2011], and the wind over the quake-damaged nuclear complex was blowing south on March 14 toward the capital, Tokyo, 240 kilometers south.

> Japan's Meteorological Agency says the winds will be slow and that what has leaked so far is not expected to affect Tokyo.

But Japan's Meteorological Agency says the winds will be slow and that what has leaked so far is not expected to affect Tokyo.

On March 12, an explosion blew the roof off of the nuclear plant's Reactor No. 1 after the earthquake triggered an automatic shutdown of all six reactors.

Diesel-powered emergency backup generators were meant to keep the reactor cores cool during the emergency shutdown. But those generators were flooded and knocked out when the tsunami struck the facility on the northeastern coast of Japan, leaving only emergency batteries to run the cooling system.

Cabinet Secretary Yukio Edano says it appears that an earlier explosion on March 14 in Reactor No. 3 was triggered when the backup battery power became depleted there and authorities pumped in seawater in a desperate attempt to keep the core from overheating.

"The explosion was believed to be the same sort of explosion as at the Reactor No. 1," Edano said. "We had issued an evacuation order for people living within a 20-kilometer radius of the plant and [now] we have told people who were in the process of evacuating to go indoors immediately."

Photo on previous page: The Fukushima Daiichi nuclear plant is seen via satellite image on March 14, 2011. The earthquake and subsequent tsunami critically damaged the reactors and caused multiple explosions, resulting in the release of radioactive particles into the air. (© DigitalGlobe/Getty Images.)

A Hydrogen Explosion

Kaoru Yoshida, a spokesman for Tokyo Electric Power Company, described the blast at Reactor No. 3 as a "hydrogen explosion."

"There was a large sound from Reactor No. 3 at 11:01 A.M. and white smoke rose," Yoshida said. "We think it is a hydrogen explosion."

But officials from the International Atomic Energy Agency said they do not think the concrete containment vessels around the two reactors were breached—a worst-case scenario that would lead to a major radioactive leak similar to the 1986 Chernobyl nuclear power plant disaster in what was then Soviet Ukraine.

> Several European countries have announced measures to revise their atomic energy policies in the wake of the crisis.

In Brussels, the European Commission called an emergency meeting of all 27 energy ministers in the European Union [EU] for March 15 to discuss nuclear safety in the wake of Japan's power plant disaster.

EU Energy Commissioner Gunther Oettinger also has invited national nuclear safety authorities and nuclear power plant operators from across the EU to discuss safety requirements for earthquakes and emergency power supply systems for reactor cooling.

Several European countries have announced measures to revise their atomic energy policies in the wake of the crisis.

German Chancellor Angela Merkel said a decision made last year [2010] to extend the life of the country's 17 nuclear power stations would be suspended for three months. A previous government decided a decade ago to shut all 17 German nuclear plants by 2021, but Merkel's administration in 2010 moved to extend their lives by an average 12 years.

Switzerland suspended its plans to build and replace nuclear plants, while Austria's environment minister

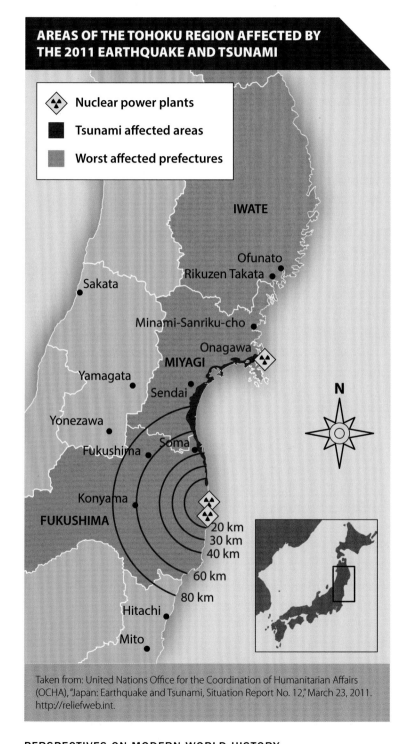

AREAS OF THE TOHOKU REGION AFFECTED BY
THE 2011 EARTHQUAKE AND TSUNAMI

Nuclear power plants

Tsunami affected areas

Worst affected prefectures

IWATE

Ofunato
Rikuzen Takata

Sakata

Minami-Sanriku-cho

Onagawa
MIYAGI

Yamagata

Sendai

Yonezawa

Soma

Fukushima

N

Konyama

FUKUSHIMA

20 km
30 km
40 km

60 km

80 km

Hitachi

Mito

Taken from: United Nations Office for the Coordination of Humanitarian Affairs
(OCHA), "Japan: Earthquake and Tsunami, Situation Report No. 12," March 23, 2011.
http://reliefweb.int.

called for atomic stress tests to make sure Europe's nuclear facilities are "earthquake-proof."

The disaster in Japan also is expected to trigger debate on the lifespan of nuclear reactors. The quake-damaged Fukushima power plant was built 40 years ago and had only one more month of operation in its current lifespan before requiring a new permit to continue operations for another 20 years. Authorities who issue those permits say they halted the permit renewal process for Fukushima on March 14.

The Disaster Causes Widespread Suffering

Meanwhile, millions of people spent a third night without water, food, or heating in near-freezing temperatures along the devastated northeastern coast. There have been more than 150 aftershocks since the March 11 quake.

Rescue workers were using chainsaws and hand picks today to dig out bodies from coastal towns devastated by the earthquake and tsunami as the official death toll from the disaster climbs.

Some 2,000 bodies were discovered along the northeastern coastline on March 14—victims of the tsunami. That raises the official death toll from the disaster to more than 2,800. But tens of thousands of people are still missing—including 18,000 people from one town there.

Japan also is suffering economically as a result of the disasters with share prices on the Tokyo Stock Exchange plunging today due to investors' fears of huge losses by Japanese industries—including global companies like Toyota and Honda.

Toxic Truth About Japan's "Miracle"

Richard Jones

In the following viewpoint, a journalist for a British periodical reports on post-tsunami Japan. A little more than three months after the earthquake, tsunami, and the nuclear crisis, it appears that much of the physical damage has been dealt with, and life is going on as it did before the March 2011 disasters. Some say Japan's recovery is best described as a modern miracle accomplishable in great part because of the Japanese belief in and dedication to *wa*, or harmony. The truth, the author argues, is that while *wa* helped the people deal with their problems, Japan is not harmonious. People are suffering the deprivations and changes mentally and silently. The government has been accused of not providing the people enough food or information and of not understanding their needs. Many think their government has failed them, he reports. This, more than anything, has led to a loss of *wa*. Richard Jones is a British photojournalist.

SOURCE. Richard Jones, "Toxic Truth About Japan's 'Miracle': Post-Tsunami Harmony Is a Myth and the Reality Is Startlingly Different," *The Mail on Sunday,* June 18, 2011. Copyright © 2011 by The Mail on Sunday. All rights reserved. Reproduced by permission.

It is an inimitable picture of Japanese order and contentment. Passengers throng Sendai Airport. In the fields and market gardens close by, farmers are tending their crops. In the city, the bullet trains are spitting out businessmen.

It is almost impossible to imagine the colossal earthquake that unleashed first a tsunami and then a nuclear nightmare just 100 days ago.

The north-eastern seaboard was devastated. Some 28,000 people are dead or missing. Sixteen towns, 95,000 buildings and 23 railway stations have been destroyed. The town of Minamisanriku has simply vanished.

No wonder the recovery, so meticulously documented in the media, has been described as a modern miracle. Today, the ships that balanced on tower blocks have gone. The debris has vanished from whole villages and towns.

It is further proof, we are reminded, that Japan is a society of immeasurable strength. And for this it can thank 'wa', or harmony. This is a collective feeling close to a sense of perfection. It ensures everyone knows their place and acts accordingly. Or so the Japanese like to tell themselves—and the outside world.

Yet post-tsunami Japan is far from harmonious. The bullet trains may be running, but in the fishing villages and tiny ports that litter the jagged coastline north of Sendai, thousands are surviving on aid handouts. The emergency cash promised by the government is yet to arrive.

> There is no doubt that 'wa' helped Japan to deal with its monumental problems; but it also means that victims suffer in silence.

Take Minamisanriku, the town whose devastating fate was pictured on the front page of *The Mail* on Sunday. There has been no miracle here. Today, it remains a nightmare of twisted metal and fragments of First World comfort. The raging 98ft wave caused annihilation. Harmony has long disappeared from Ishinomaki, too. The port town, 30 miles from Sendai, took the full force of the tsunami. It is a ghost town shrouded in the stench of rotting fish.

There is no doubt that 'wa' helped Japan to deal with its monumental problems; but it also means that victims suffer in silence. In the immediate aftermath of the tsunami, orderly queues snaked for miles for food, water and fuel. There was no looting and raping, which often accompanies natural disasters elsewhere.

Now, though, victims break down when I meet them. Mother-of-two Mrs Hiroake has lived with her family on two mats in an evacuation shelter in Ishinomaki since the tsunami hit.

'We are living in a limbo with no privacy,' she says. 'Our lives stopped. People here are suffering mentally.'

The 254 billion yen (£1.94 billion) raised by the Japanese Red Cross for tsunami victims (including £10.5 million donated from Britain) is taking an astonishingly long time to reach the people who need it most. Just 37 billion yen has been distributed so far.

Pensions and welfare payments, too, have dried up. Mr Konno, a diabetic, can't understand why his monthly benefits of 15,000 yen (£114) stopped the moment he moved to a shelter.

Another victim, a 78-year-old widow, Mrs Utako Saito, sleeps in a tent she has pitched in her wrecked wooden cottage. She has not received her pension for three months.

With unemployment running at 90 per cent, the needy are starting to revolt. One third of families are refusing to move to temporary housing, opting to remain in shelters to hang onto their precious food benefits. Sixty per cent of the 28,000 temporary homes remain unoccupied. A staggering 90,000 people remain in shelters.

'The government don't want people to get too comfortable here, so they don't allow evacuees electricity inside the shelter,' says a volunteer from the Catholic charity Caritas.

However, the worst affected may prove to be those who lost nothing in the way of homes or relatives. They may have no running water, no money, no employment. But when compensation is finally awarded, they will be entitled to nothing.

The large hill-top home of Chieko Miura, 62, just north of Minamisanriku, became a shelter for 30 locals.

'Eventually we managed to get rice balls from the government, but there was nothing for my family because we were not "victims,"' Mrs Miura, who still looks after 12 evacuees, recalls.

'This government can be very cold-hearted. Do they want us to abandon the people we are helping?'

Tears are streaming down her face as she says this, and she apologises. Survivors have been eating little more than biscuits and dried food.

'Should we take the home with no food or stay in the shelter and eat?' says Mrs Miaki, 46, a sea-urchin fisherman, at Yariki Bay, north of Sendai.

According to Kei Watabe, who distributes food, people are not starving, 'but they are not getting enough food from the government. Japan is not the Third World. This is not Africa. The Japanese government are the first to send aid overseas, but when it comes to their own people they are blind.'

If these tsunami victims have been deprived of food, the rest of Japan has been starved of information. The Japanese are now struggling to comprehend how their government could mislead them about the nuclear meltdown that followed the tsunami.

When the Fukushima nuclear plant exploded on March 12, and again two days later, Tokyo Electric Power Company (TEPCO), the plant's operator, the government and the media, reassured the nation, and the world, that everything was under control.

It was not until May 12 that officials conceded that there had been a meltdown at not one, but three reactors. Even the timing of the announcement was cynical. It happened as inspectors from the International Atomic Energy Agency (IAEA) were about to arrive.

Rescue workers search for survivors in the wreckage in the small town of Minamisanriku on March 15, 2011. (© Jiji Press/AFP/Getty Images.)

TEPCO was able to control information through the age-old system of Press Clubs, where the government provides information to selected media.

But *The Mail* on Sunday spoke to sources inside the Japanese nuclear industry who knew that radiation readings spiked 155 miles south of Fukushima, immediately after the first explosion. They were told by officials to keep the findings quiet.

A survey by Fuji Television Network last month found that 81 per cent of the public no longer trusts any government information about radiation.

Food shopping has also become a problem. Shops have started mixing vegetables from different prefectures as customers are now selecting food based on where it is grown.

In an attempt to reassure the nation, the Japanese Prime Minister, Naoto Kan, visited Fukushima last month where he cheerfully ate locally grown cherries and tomatoes in front of the news cameras. As he spoke, bulldozers were removing the top soil from Fukushima school playgrounds due to high radiation levels.

Michael Penn, president of the Shingetsu News Agency, says: 'The media and the government share a cultural inclination to keep the people calm. But this time the government have badly misunderstood the public's needs.'

It is not the first time that the government and bureaucrats have neglected public safety. In the early Nineties around 1,800 people developed AIDS after being infected with untreated blood products. Most victims were dead before the Ministry of Health admitted negligence.

According to a well-known Japanese documentary maker, TEPCO paid for the creation of a blacklist of actors and musicians who are against the nuclear industry.

When one actor, Taro Yamamoto, joined an anti-nuclear protest, he lost his part in a popular soap opera. Yamamoto's 'crime' was to say that schoolchildren in Fukushima should not be subjected to the same annual

> "A survey by Fuji Television Network last month found that 81 per cent of the public no longer trusts any government information about radiation."

radiation dose (20 microsieverts per year) as nuclear power workers in Europe.

One hundred days after the biggest earthquake in Japanese history, life is certainly not back to normal. One refugee told me: 'My biggest worry is that the people here will be forgotten as the media focus on the nuclear crisis.'

And 'wa', the harmony, is disappearing as people feel that their government has failed them.

As Japan's Tsunami Debris Arrives, Can the US West Coast Handle It?

Winston Ross

In the following viewpoint, a US journalist reports on the arrival on US West Coast beaches of debris from the tsunami that struck Japan more than a year and a half earlier. The first piece of debris—a huge dock—landed on an Oregon beach. It came earlier than expected and made extra work for the state park officials who managed the beach. When the northerly winds of summer switch to the southerly winds of winter, all sorts of tsunami debris will hit the West Coast shores. Thus far, the debris has drawn tourists and debris-seeking beachcombers to the areas where it has landed, led to more frequent state beach cleanups, and had an impact on state budgets. Winston Ross is a national correspondent for *Newsweek* and *The Daily Beast*.

In the coming weeks and months [fall 2012], a weather phenomenon known as the "fall transition" will wash the artifacts of a national tragedy onto West Coast beaches.

The fall transition happens when the Northern Hemisphere storm track that governs prevailing winds sends those gusts in a completely different direction—from south to north and from offshore to inland—along with stuff that gets pushed around in the water. Right now, among the stuff that's floating offshore is a whirlpool of junk known as the Pacific Gyre, which is estimated to hold 5 million pounds of bashed-in houses, fishing boats, docks, and dead bodies from the March 11, 2011, tsunami in Japan. The more buoyant relics of this disaster have been bobbing along for 18 months, with a few notable exceptions that have left state and federal officials scrambling to respond.

Finding Tsunami Debris

When a massive dock thunked its way onto Oregon's Agate Beach this summer, pandemonium ensued. Not only was the thing huge—at 66 feet long, 8 feet tall, and 165 tons—it was covered in gnarly invasive species, and had script in Kanji on a small plaque at the bottom. After a little sleuthing by Portland's Japanese consulate, everyone's worst fears were confirmed: the first piece of debris from last spring's disaster had finally hit the continental U.S., much sooner than anyone had expected.

> When a massive dock thunked its way onto Oregon's Agate Beach this summer, pandemonium ensued.

Overnight, the "tsunami dock" became an instant tourist attraction and a headache for state parks officials, who manage the beach. They dispatched rangers in mostly futile attempts to keep rambunctious youngsters from turning the thing into a jungle gym, and they

Three months after the earthquake and tsunami struck Japan's coast, a massive dock with Japanese writing washed ashore on Agate Beach, Oregon. (© AP Images/ Rick Bowmer.)

puzzled back in Salem about how to get rid of it, and how to pay for that.

Two months and $85,000 later, the dock was gone. A contractor cut it into pieces using a Rube Goldberg-looking contraption whereby a diamond saw looped around and under it and sliced. This was a huge disappointment to the fans who painted a mural on the side. But it was the only option, insisted those that run the Oregon Parks and Recreation Department. You can't just leave stuff on the beach, they said. It sets a terrible precedent.

Over the next few months, Oregon and the rest of the West Coast will find that argument bolstered—by a need to keep the landing strip clear. The dock did indeed arrive early, months ahead of schedule, likely shoved faster than the currents would otherwise have carried it thanks to "windage," an uncannily appropriate term used to describe how much of a thing is sticking out of the water, how much it creates a kind of accidental sail. The dock actually sailed across the Pacific, in other words, as much as it did float.

Which is to say there's much more tsunami debris—with less windage—still out there. Of the 5 million tons of debris estimated to have washed into the ocean after the March 2011 quake, Japanese officials say 70 percent of it sank. The rest floated. There are two more docks, just like the one the state just spent four years of college tuition to remove. There are plastic bottles, fishing floats, lightbulbs, giant chunks of Styrofoam, small appliances, mannequin parts, buoys, even entire fishing vessels. A few weeks after the dock showed up in Oregon, a 20-foot fiberglass boat covered in pelagic gooseneck barnacles up to 3 feet long washed up at Cape Disappointment State Park, in Washington. The boat was also traced to the tsunami, Curt Hart of the Washington Department of Ecology told *The Daily Beast*. After determining that the owner "didn't want it back," the state checked it for radiation (all clear), blasted it clean and tossed it in a landfill.

Marine debris is not a new phenomenon. Litterbugs and careless ship crewmen and leaking landfills have conspired for decades to clog the world's oceans with all sorts of junk, creating loosely affiliated "garbage patches" in certain gyres with clockwise, rotating currents that have a way of concentrating marine debris. That problem is the raison d'être for The 5 Gyres Institute, a Los Angeles-based nonprofit whose founders have spent much of the past three years sailing the world's oceans with a "Manta Trawl" attached to the side of the boat, scooping up samples of trash so as to generate estimates of how much more is out there.

It's frustrating for 5 Gyres' policy coordinator Stiv Wilson to be reminded that people don't seem to know how rubbish-laden the planet's waterways actually are. "All these images, such stunning images when the tsunami first happened, the same pictures exist of what a river in Jakarta looks like every day," he told *The Daily Beast*.

Still, the tsunami debris has presented Wilson and other conservationists with a rare opportunity. The Agate Beach dock inspired tens of thousands of tourists to flock there and get a glimpse of it and that's not a fad that will fade just because the dock is gone. Beachcombers who have long pored over Oregon's shores for interesting stuff now have an entirely new mission: find tsunami debris. Bear witness to a piece of history. "These are the artifacts of human lives," Wilson said. . . .

> "Tsunami debris has presented . . . conservationists with a rare opportunity."

A Rise in Beach Cleanups

And it's up to state parks officials and conservationists alike to remind people what to do with that stuff—providing, of course, that they don't want to keep it. Beach cleanups organized by the Oregon chapter of the Surfrider Foundation have doubled in frequency since the tsunami dock arrived, and the number of people calling to participate in them has skyrocketed, said Gus Gates, the nonprofit's policy manager. Calls to the state beach-cleanup coordinators have numbered in the thousands.

"Everyone I talk to, they're still looking for the next Harley to wash up," Gates said, referring to the Harley-Davidson motorcycle—still in its shipping container—that washed up on a British Columbia beach this year. "They're thinking they might find something like that. Something cool."

This is the happy ending to a twofold tragedy: the devastating tsunami itself, and the trash that was already in the ocean long before the earth started shaking in Japan last year. Most tsunami debris won't be readily identifiable as such. It's just ordinary household items.

Whether it's trash or historical artifact, though, people will still be picking it up. Still throwing it away, wiping the beaches clean of anything else they see, and they're being reminded as they do so of just how permanent those little plastic water and soda bottles are, how they live forever.

> "In Washington . . . crews cleaned 57 miles of beach, end to end."

"You can't really tell if it's tsunami debris or just trash," Gates said. "But it doesn't belong there."

It's a treasure hunt-turned-community-service project. In Washington, after the boat washed up in June, crews cleaned 57 miles of beach, end to end, Hart said.

"The beaches in the southern part of the state never seemed so clean," he said.

Mobilizing to Pick Up Debris

It's also an art project. On Oregon's southern coast, in Bandon, Angela Haseltine Pozzi has long been collecting trash and turning it into sculpture at the nonprofit Washed Ashore. Now, she's expecting an influx of new material. She's planning an exhibit dedicated to the tsunami victims and using its debris. And she realizes she needs to be careful about how to pull that off.

"A lot of people are interested, amazed, horrified by the imagery," Pozzi said. "To actually see that thing, to make that connection, it has to be done in a very sensitive way."

Pozzi says Washed Ashore uses every last bit of material it collects. The tsunami debris is different, not just because it comes from Japan, but because it includes "a huge amount of Styrofoam." That'll force her to adapt the art, she said, probably by replacing the recycled welded steel framework she now uses as a hollow structure with Styrofoam as a base.

It's a good thing that volunteers have mobilized to pick up tsunami debris—there's little in the way of funds coming from the states or federal government. NOAA

[National Oceanic and Atmospheric Administration] has provided each of the three West Coast states with $50,000 for cleanup; in Oregon, that's a tenth of what the state has spent so far on tsunami debris. NOAA spokeswoman Keeley Belva said the agency has done some concerted marine-debris cleanups—a recent research expedition in the northwest Hawaiian Islands, for example, netted 50 tons of material—but the tsunami debris is spread out across an area that is three times as big as the continental U.S. There's little the agency can do but monitor it, and tell people what to do when they find it.

> "It's a good thing that volunteers have mobilized to pick up tsunami debris—there's little in the way of funds coming from the states or federal government."

"Who could possibly manage it?" said Al Pazar, a crab fisherman from Florence, Ore., who doesn't run his boat at night "unless absolutely necessary" because of the debris. "It's in God's hands."

Soon, currents and winds that now head north-to-south will switch, pushing debris on shore. Unwieldy trash piles or not, the coming treasure hunts are sure to be interesting ones. In April, a soccer ball turned up on a remote Alaskan island with Japanese writing on it. The beachcombers who found it traced the ball to a school and actually got it back to the owner, 16-year-old Misaki Murakami. The boy had lost everything in the disaster, and was glad to have it back. His classmates had given it to him in 2005.

On it, the students wrote "Hang in there, Murakami!!"

I Am One of the Fukushima Fifty

David McNeill

The author of the following viewpoint reports on an interview with one of the Tokyo Electric Power Company (TEPCO) employees who volunteered to return to the Fukushima Daiichi nuclear power plant after it had been hit by the March 11, 2011, earthquake and tsunami. He describes the damage caused by the natural disasters and shares the conditions the worker and his colleagues endured while trying to stop the catastrophe at the plant. The author comments on the effects of the disaster, the lack of public acknowledgement of the volunteers, and TEPCO's role in the meltdown. David McNeill is the Japan correspondent for the *Chronicle of Higher Education* and writes regularly for *The Independent*, the *Irish Times*, and *Japan Times*. He is an *Asia-Pacific Journal* coordinator and coauthor of the highly acclaimed book about Japan's 2011 disasters, *Strong in the Rain*.

It was, recalls Atsufumi Yoshizawa, a suicide mission: volunteering to return to a dangerously radioactive nuclear power plant on the verge of tipping out of control.

As he said goodbye to his colleagues they saluted him, like soldiers in battle. The wartime analogies were hard to avoid: in the international media he was a kamikaze, a samurai or simply one of the heroic Fukushima 50. The descriptions still embarrass him. "I'm not a hero," he says. "I was just trying to do my job."

A stoic, soft-spoken man dressed in the blue utility suit of his embattled employer Tokyo Electric Power Co., (Tepco) Mr Yoshizawa still finds it hard to dredge up memories of fighting to stop catastrophe at the Fukushima Daiichi plant. Two years later, debate still rages about responsibility for the planet's worst nuclear disaster since Chernobyl [1986], and its impact. Fish caught near the plant this month contained over 5,000 times safe radiation limits, according to state broadcaster NHK.

A report this week [March 2, 2013] by the World Health Organisation says female infants affected by the worst of the fallout have a 70 per cent higher risk of developing thyroid cancer over their lifetimes, but concluded that overall risks for the rest of the population are "low". Over 160,000 people have been displaced from their homes near the plant, perhaps permanently, and are fighting for proper compensation. Stress, divorce and suicides plague the evacuees.

> Mr Yoshizawa says he feels 'deep responsibility' for the crisis his company triggered.

Mr Yoshizawa says he feels "deep responsibility" for the crisis his company triggered. His eyes brim with tears at points in his story, which begins with the magnitude-9 quake less than 100 miles away from the plant under the sea on 11 March 2011. "It was so strong I fell on my hands and knees," says the 54-year-old engineer. "There was no place to hide."

The quake's shockwaves ripped pipes from walls, bounced parked cars like toys and budded roads at the 864-acre plant. Initially, Mr Yoshizawa believed the Dai-ichi's defensive engineering had worked. The instant the tremors struck, control rods were automatically inserted into the plant's three working reactors to shut down nuclear fission, a process known as "scram." But the shaking had cut power from the main electricity grid, probably damaged the cooling system to reactor one, and a destructive tsunami over twice as high as the plant's defences was just 49 minutes away.

Mr Yoshizawa was in charge of reactors five and six, which at the time were shut down for maintenance. He ran to the plant's seismic isolation building and took his post beside manager Masao Yoshida, who was trying to assess the damage. In the windowless bunker they couldn't see the tsunami that hit the complex. Waves of 13 to 15 metres high washed over the 5.7m sea wall. Water flooded the basements of the turbine buildings, on the ocean side of the reactors, shorting out electric switching units and disabling 12 of the 13 emergency generators and then backup batteries, the last line of defence. There was no power to pump water to the nuclear core and carry off the heat, or even measure the radiation. The engineers had lost control over the complex. Meltdown had begun.

Mr Yoshizawa recalls hearing the first reports inside the bunker of oil tanks and cars floating in water outside. "I just couldn't imagine a tsunami that big," he says. The crisis quickly deepened. Just over 15 hours after the power loss, uranium fuel melted through the pressure vessel of reactor number one. Units two and three were not far behind. Thousands fled from nearby towns and villages. There was no plan for what to do next because Tepco had never predicted total loss of power at a plant.

Most of Daiichi's employees had gone home to check on their families. Mr Yoshizawa says he thought of two things: "The safety of my workers, and the complete shutdown of the power plant." His own wife and two daughters were safe in Yokohama, hundreds of miles south. There was no question of panic, or running back to see them, he insists. "It might seem strange to others, but it's natural for us to put our company first. It's part of the mind and spirit of Tepco workers to deal with emergencies."

The engineer says he moved offsite for a few days to a disaster-response building in the town of Okuma, 5 km away. But on 15 and 16 March 2011 the situation at Daiichi reached its most critical phase. A series of hydrogen explosions had left much of the complex a tangled mess of radioactive concrete and steel. Unit three had exploded, three reactors were in meltdown and over 1000 fuel rods in the reactor four building, normally covered under 16 feet of water, had boiled dry, raising the spectre of a nuclear fission chain reaction. In his darkest moments, Mr Yoshizawa admits he shared the same fear as other experts—that the crisis could also trigger the evacuation of the Fukushima Daini plant 10 km away.

> About 250 km south in Tokyo, the government feared a nightmare scenario: a vast toxic cloud heading toward the world's most populated metropolis.

About 250 km south in Tokyo, the government feared a nightmare scenario: a vast toxic cloud heading toward the world's most populated metropolis. Rumours swirled that Tepco was preparing to completely pull out its staff from the Daiichi plant, leaving it to spin out of control. Mr Yoshizawa denies this. "We never intended to abandon our jobs," he insists. "At the time that rumour was circulating I was volunteering to go back." He recalls despairing at the situation. "Most people thought we would not be coming back from the plant," he says, on the verge

In May 2012, employees of the Tokyo Electric Power Company (TEPCO) escort members of the media around the site of the destroyed nuclear reactor at Fukushima Daiichi. (© Tomohiro Ohsumi/AFP/Getty Images.)

of tears. In the media the Fukushima 50 was born, although Mr Yoshizawa says that in reality there were 70 of them, mostly in their middle age. "We had all resolved to stay till the end."

Throughout the following weeks on the frontline of the crisis, the men endured brutal conditions. Deliveries stalled, food almost ran out and water was restricted to a single 500ml bottle every two days. Working in shifts, surviving on biscuits and sleeping when he could inside the radiation-proofed bunker, Mr Yoshizawa lost weight and grew a beard. As elite firefighters succeeded in getting water to the overheating reactors, the collective psyche inside the bunker lightened and the dreaded words "oshimai da" (it's the end), were no longer heard. Exhausted and dishevelled on his first trip back to a sunny Tokyo a month after the quake, he was startled to find life going on as normal.

Public recognition or even gratitude for the ordeal endured by Mr Yoshizawa and his colleagues is scarce. Most are still employed by a company disgraced by revelations that it had repeatedly ignored pre-March 11 warnings about the risks of natural disaster. Taxpayers will have to bear the cost of cleaning up from the accident after Tepco was nationalised last year. Not a single manager has been held accountable for what happened.

> "Public recognition or even gratitude for the ordeal endured by Mr Yoshizawa and his colleagues is scarce."

The utility's rehabilitation has been hampered by fresh stories that it had misled investigators before an on-site check of reactor one, lying that the reactor building was "too dark" for inspection. Some critics suspect the company was trying to conceal evidence of damage from the earthquake, an issue with potentially profound implications for restarting Japan's 50 commercial reactors, most of which are shut down.

It took the government 18 months to publicly acknowledge Mr Yoshizawa and his comrades, when then Prime Minister Yoshihiko Noda officially thanked them last October. Most were not identified or even named, testimony both to the trauma Fukushima has inflicted on Japan's collective psyche, and a deep-seated cultural reluctance to grandstand while others suffer. Some of the men fear reprisals or bullying of their children in school. A police van is permanently parked outside the company's headquarters in Tokyo. Tepco itself is reluctant to wheel the Fukushima 50 out in front of the media, for fear of what they might reveal about what happened—Mr Yoshizawa is shadowed throughout his interviews by a PR minder.

But if he nurses any bitterness toward his employer, he never reveals it. He praises the company for providing counseling to the ex-Daiichi workers and regular health checks—a select list of employees who absorbed poten-

The Accident at Chernobyl

In the wan light of a snowy spring morning, belongings scattered on the floor of an abandoned kindergarten speak of a time before the children of Pripyat [Ukraine] lost their innocence. . . .

Before dawn on April 26, 1986, less than two miles . . . south of what was then a city of 50,000, the Chernobyl Nuclear Power Plant's number four reactor exploded. Thirty people died in the blast and fire or were exposed to lethal radiation. The destroyed hulk burned for ten days, contaminating tens of thousands of square miles in northern Ukraine, southern Belarus, and Russia's Bryansk region. It was the worst nuclear accident the world has ever seen.

The fallout, 400 times more radioactivity than was released at Hiroshima, drove a third of a million people from their homes and triggered an epidemic of thyroid cancer in children. Over the years, the economic losses . . . have mounted into the hundreds of billions of dollars. As evidence of government bungling and secrecy emerged in its wake, Chernobyl (or Chornobyl, as it is now known in independent Ukraine) even sped the breakup of the Soviet Union.

SOURCE. *Richard Stone, "The Long Shadow of Chernobyl," National Geographic, April 2006, pp. 1–2.*

tially harmful amounts of radiation are qualified for unlimited aftercare. His own final tally of internal exposure was 50 millisieverts—the upper annual limit in the US for nuclear plant workers.

Now dealing with waste and fuel management, and back at Tepco headquarters, he says the work at the plant has far from ended. "Nobody has any experience of trying to safely extract nuclear fuel after such an accident," he says. British and US engineers are helping in a collective effort that will take many years. He gets uncomfortable when he returns to Fukushima and has to remember the crisis. His family never discusses what happened. "My wife and children have already seen so much on TV and they don't want to see or hear anything more about it. Occasionally they will ask me if I'm OK and I tell them what I tell you: I don't have any problems."

Living in Limbo: Refugees' Grievances

Two years on, thousands of people forced to leave their homes in the wake of the Fukushima disaster are living in limbo, yet to receive compensation and unable to move back owing to dangerous radiation.

More than 160,000 people were forcibly evacuated from the area when an earthquake and tsunami crippled the Fukushima Daiichi nuclear plant on 11 March 2011, and tens of thousands left voluntarily.

Tokyo Electric Power (Tepco), the company that owns the plant, has paid compensation to some nuclear refugees, including what it calls "temporary" compensation for living costs, but it has paid no money for assets damaged by the meltdown.

A recent report by Greenpeace documented a litany of complaints about complicated forms, insufficient living costs and low valuations on property. Greenpeace said the plan was drawn up by Tepco in July last year [2012] and is based on a "complex and disputed" government system.

CHAPTER 2

Controversies Surrounding Japan's 2011 Natural Disasters and Nuclear Meltdown

Japan Prepared Well for Tsunamis

Andrew Moore

Photo on previous page: A destroyed fire truck lies amid other debris in Minamisoma, Fukushima, Japan, north of the disabled nuclear power plant. The scale of the destruction hampered rescue and relief efforts. (© **Sankei**/**Getty Images.**)

In the following viewpoint, an academic who spent two years working in a Japanese research laboratory that studied natural disasters maintains that Japan is the most disaster-aware nation in the world. No other country, he proclaims, has an earthquake warning system equal to Japan's or a coastline as well protected against tsunamis as Japan's northern coastline. He explains that one of the first scientific studies of a tsunami took place in Japan, and the nation has been putting measures in place for a century to protect against disasters like those that struck on March 11, 2011. The 2011 disaster is the first real test of the various technologies put in place. It will show what works and what does not. Andrew Moore is an assistant professor of geology at Earlham College in Indiana and served as a tsunami researcher in Japan from 1999 to 2001.

SOURCE. Andrew Moore, "Japan Prepared Well for Tsunami," CNN Opinion, March 11, 2011. Copyright © 2011 by Andrew Moore. All rights reserved. Reproduced by permission.

L ike many around the world, I sit transfixed by the images coming this morning from northern Japan, where a devastating earthquake and tsunami have already claimed hundreds of lives. It has a special resonance for me because I lived in Sendai, in the Tohoku region, from 1999 to 2001, working in a Japanese research laboratory dedicated to the study and control of natural disasters. I was a tsunami researcher in that lab.

Japan is arguably the most disaster-aware nation in the world, and has spent several decades developing mitigation strategies for a variety of hazards, including earthquakes and tsunamis. The area struck by this event is really where such studies began, and as a result, it represents the state of the art in readiness for earthquake and tsunami disasters.

The earthquake early warning system there is unparalleled. In place only since late 2007, the system effectively "outruns" the earthquake. Ideally, information about the shock is transmitted to people—there are few populations as wired as Japan's—even before the damaging earthquake waves arrive. At best, this system provides up to about 10 seconds of warning in affected regions, and of course works best farther from the epicenter.

Much of northern Japan remains without power, so it remains to be seen if the system, which was triggered, arrived in time to provide a useful warning.

The Impact of Tsunamis on the Northern Coast of Japan

The coastline of northern Japan is a special one—north of Sendai, the coast becomes steep, rocky and deeply embayed. It's a rugged coast, where small fishing towns sit at the backs of bays. As a result, wave and tsunami energy focuses on them.

An 1896 tsunami killed over 10,000 people in these villages, in some cases eradicating entire towns. In

In the town of Taro on March 23, 2011, a woman walks across a seawall that was designed to protect the low-lying city from a tsunami. (© Roslan Rahman/AFP/Getty Images.)

part because of that event, Japan's northern coastline is perhaps the best protected area in the world against tsunamis. Ten-meter high walls defend many towns. Road signs mark the beginning and end of inundation areas determined as such by sophisticated computer simulations. Evacuation routes are well-signed, and vertical evacuation is available in areas distant from high ground. Greenbelts designed to dissipate tsunami energy line most of the coast.

In truth, one of the first scientific studies of a tsunami happened here. After the 1896 event, a tsunami survey was commissioned by the government, and a

What Causes a Tsunami

Large earthquakes under or near the ocean that produce vertical movements of the seafloor will generate a tsunami. The 9.0 magnitude earthquake that struck off Japan's northern coast on March 11, 2011, was that kind of earthquake. When its energy was transferred to the water column above it, the result was a tsunami, or seismic sea wave. The tsunami rose up to 135 feet above sea level. When the waves reached the shallow water of Japan's coastline, their force was increased, and the tsunami swamped everything in its path.

If you go to a beach and look out at the ocean, you will see waves. Those waves are caused by the wind blowing across the surface of the ocean. Generally the time between two of the waves, known as a period, ranges from five to twenty seconds. A tsunami period, however, can range from ten minutes to two hours. Another difference has to do with the distance between two identical points, or wavelength. On a normal ocean wave it is roughly 100 meters [328 feet]. On a tsunami it is up to 500 kilometers [310.6 miles].

Tsunamis happen suddenly, generally without any warning and consist of a series of waves. The first wave is not necessarily the largest, so it is a mistake to think it will be safe after the first large wave passes. The danger is present until after all the waves have passed, which may take hours.

report written—still available today—that laid out what these first researchers felt helped people survive. The evacuation routes and coastal greenbelts date from this early study, as does perhaps the earliest tsunami public education program: The Japanese government commissioned the carving of several stone monuments describing the event and had them placed throughout the affected area.

In short, the northern coast of Japan represents the best that's out there right now to help detect and survive earthquakes and tsunamis. Much of this technology is relatively new: The concrete barriers are mostly from the mid 1980s, and the road signs were put in place more recently, as has the concept of vertical evacuation—building tall tsunami resistant structures in low-lying areas.

So, as this disaster plays out, and as we wait to hear if friends and old neighbors are OK, I think the larger question we'll want to ask is: Do the measures we've put in place over the last 100 years work?

This event is the first real test we'll see for all of the various technologies we use to protect people in tsunamis. Some of them probably worked well, and others appear to have failed—determining which will be part of the recovery effort.

> "In short, the northern coast of Japan represents the best that's out there right now to help detect and survive earthquakes and tsunamis.

Thousands Died Because Japan Was Not Prepared for the Tsunami

Bruce Parker

In the following viewpoint, a visiting professor at the Center for Maritime Systems argues that the tsunami death rate was so high chiefly because the Japanese people did not have the necessary tsunami preparedness training. Many did not know what to do if a tsunami came and were unable to react quickly enough, he asserts. Another factor was that people had put too much confidence in the measures supposedly in place to protect them. When the tsunami hit, he maintains, some of these measures proved lacking, such as seawalls that had been built too low to hold back the water and evacuation areas not up high enough or not far enough inland. Bruce Parker is a former chief scientist for the National Ocean Service in the National Oceanic and Atmospheric Administration, a former director of the World Data Center for Oceanography, and author of *The Power of the Sea: Tsunamis, Storm Surges, Rogue Waves, and Our Quest to Predict Disasters*.

SOURCE. Bruce Parker, "Why Did the 2011 Japan Tsunami Kill So Many People?," *Huffington Post*, March 11, 2012. Copyright © 2012 by Bruce Parker. All rights reserved. Reproduced by permission.

That Japan was not adequately prepared for the tsunami that hit the northeastern Honshu coast on March 11, 2011, first became apparent at the Fukushima Daiichi nuclear power plant. When the earthquake severed the connection between the nuclear power plant and the Japan electrical grid, the diesel backup system turned on as it was supposed to. This was critical, because those generators provided the electrical energy needed to continue the operation of the cooling system, without which there would be a nuclear meltdown. But the sea wall in front of the power plant was not high enough to stop the tsunami, and the fuel tanks were washed away. Unbelievably those critical fuel tanks had been situated outside the buildings at ground level. Equally unbelievable, the diesel engines inside the buildings had also been placed at ground level and in the basement below, and the tsunami submerged them. (If the fuel tanks and diesel engines had simply been put on higher floors in the nuclear reactor buildings, which withstood the force of the tsunami, or the sea wall had been higher, there would have been no nuclear accident.)

> The fact that 25,000 Japanese were killed by the tsunami shows that the lack of preparation went well beyond just the nuclear power plants.

But the fact that 25,000 Japanese were killed by the tsunami shows that the lack of preparation went well beyond just the nuclear power plants. So one has to ask the question, how could the tsunami have killed so many people in a country that was supposed to be the most tsunami-aware nation on Earth?

A Mixture of Complacency and Overconfidence

Part of the answer is that the Japanese had become complacent about tsunamis and over-confident about the measures supposedly in place to protect them. Although there had been many recent earthquakes, there had not been a deadly large tsunami since 1933. And people forget. In 1960 the tsunami from the Chilean earthquake that had crossed the Pacific and reached Japan killed 142 people. But since then there had only been false alarms, tsunami warnings broadcast but followed by no tsunamis of any significant size. And the fact that the Japanese had made very real progress in reducing deaths due to the frequent earthquakes (better building codes, etc.) added further to their false sense of security about tsunamis.

The Japanese thought the sea walls would protect them. About 40 percent of the coast of Japan has sea walls, but unfortunately they had not been built high enough and they failed to protect the people on March 11. How high to build those walls had been a financial decision. It would have been much more expensive to build them high enough to handle a worst-case scenario, which the March 11 tsunami was, produced by a 9.0 earthquake, the fifth largest in modern history. (Of course, if there was one place where the highest and strongest sea wall should have been built, to handle a worst case scenario, no matter what the cost, it was around the nuclear reactors.) There is, however, very little cost associated with designating safe evacuation areas. Surprisingly, many of these supposedly safe evacuation areas were not located high enough and/or far enough inland, and many people who came to these evacuation areas died. Perhaps most important, however, many of the deaths were due to the fact that a large number of Japanese did not know what to do if a tsunami came. They had been trained in earthquake preparedness, but not in tsunami preparedness.

The Importance of Tsunami Preparedness Training

The tsunami struck in the middle of a sunny Friday afternoon at a time when thousands of parents were heading to schools to pick up their children. The stories of what happened at many elementary and junior high schools sadly provide tragic insights into the lack of preparation. However, there was one school district that was prepared, and how those children saved themselves because of their training is a very uplifting story. It is a story that demonstrates the critical importance of disaster preparedness in saving lives, especially for tsunamis, which are unpredictable. In the Kamaishi school district, only five children were lost out [of] thousands (and those five had been at home when the tsunami struck).

In 2005 Professor Toshitaka Katada, a disaster social-engineering expert at Gunma University Graduate School, and his colleagues began giving emergency disaster lessons to students at elementary and junior high schools in the Kamaishi school district. They conducted disaster drills, but they also integrated tsunami awareness into almost all aspects of their school day. The goal of the program was to teach the students to save themselves. The story of how the students from Kamaishi-Higashi Junior High School and Unosumai Elementary School saved themselves during the tsunami provides a heartwarming illustration of the benefit of tsunami preparedness training. The tsunami swept over sea walls and engulfed both schools, yet every one of the 212 junior high students and 350 elementary students who were in the buildings at the time managed to escape.

The Speed of Tsunamis and the Timing of Warnings

And what about the tsunami warnings? How quickly were they issued, and how much time did the Japanese have to react? Tsunamis are unpredictable, because the submarine earthquakes that produce them are unpredictable. Also, most submarine earthquakes do not produce tsunamis, so to prevent false alarms an actual tsunami must first be detected (by a DART [Deep-Ocean

Assesment and Reporting of Tsunami] buoy or a real-time tide gauge) before a warning can be given. This works fine for warning people living along coast[s] far from the epicenter of the submarine earthquake. (Tsunami models did an excellent job of predicting when the tsunami would hit Hawaii or California, hours after the

A temporary mass grave is filled with the simple wooden caskets of disaster victims on March 26, 2011, in Miyagi, Japan. (© **Kuni Takahashi/Getty Images.**)

earthquake.) But most deaths occur on the coast closest to the epicenter. On March 11, the very large size of the earthquake was recognized quickly (from the seismic data) and the Japanese Meteorological Agency fortunately took no chances and put out a tsunami warning three minutes later. Even so, it took only 29 minutes for the tsunami to reach the closest point on the Japanese coast.

> With so little time to try to escape, tsunami preparedness becomes the most important thing in saving lives.

With so little time to try to escape, tsunami preparedness becomes the most important thing in saving lives. Unfortunately, the response of many Japanese to that warning was inadequate due to their lack of tsunami preparedness training.

The Fukushima Nuclear Power Plant Accident Was a "Man-Made" Disaster

The National Diet of Japan Fukushima Nuclear Accident Independent Investigation Commission

In the following viewpoint, an investigation commission contends that the direct causes of the 2011 Fukushima nuclear power plant accident were the earthquake and the tsunami, not just the tsunami as claimed by the Tokyo Electric Power Company (TEPCO). The plant would have been capable of withstanding both natural disasters, concludes the commission, if TEPCO, the regulators, and the Japanese government had acted responsibly. TEPCO, for example, did not take the necessary preventive measures. The situation continued to worsen because the crisis management

SOURCE. The National Diet of Japan Fukushima Nuclear Accident Independent Investigation Commission, "Executive Summary," *The Official Report of The Fukushima Nuclear Accident Independent Investigation Commission*, 2012, pp. 16–21. Copyright © 2012 by National Diet of Japan. All rights reserved. Reproduced by permission.

system of the prime minister's office, the regulators, and other responsible agencies did not function correctly. They had neither the preparation nor the way of thinking they needed to competently operate an appropriate emergency response. The National Diet of Japan Fukushima Nuclear Accident Independent Investigation Commission was a commission formed in 2011 to investigate the cause of the Fukushima Daiichi nuclear disaster.

The direct causes of the [Fukushima Daiichi nuclear power plant] accident were all foreseeable prior to March 11, 2011. But the Fukushima Daiichi Nuclear Power Plant was incapable of withstanding the earthquake and tsunami that hit on that day. The operator (TEPCO), the regulatory bodies (NISA and NSC) and the government body promoting the nuclear power industry (METI), all failed to correctly develop the most basic safety requirements—such as assessing the probability of damage, preparing for containing collateral damage from such a disaster, and developing evacuation plans for the public in the case of a serious radiation release.

TEPCO and the Nuclear and Industrial Safety Agency (NISA) were aware of the need for structural reinforcement in order to conform to new guidelines, but rather than demanding their implementation, NISA stated that action should be taken autonomously by the operator. The Commission has discovered that no part of the required reinforcements had been implemented on Units 1 through 3 by the time of the accident. This was the result of tacit consent by NISA for a significant delay by the operators in completing the reinforcement. In addition, although NISA and the operators were aware of the risk of core damage from tsunami, no regulations were created, nor did TEPCO take any protective steps against such an occurrence.

Since 2006, the regulators and TEPCO were aware of the risk that a total outage of electricity at the Fukushima Daiichi plant might occur if a tsunami were to reach the level of the site. They were also aware of the risk of reactor core damage from the loss of seawater pumps in the case of a tsunami larger than assumed in the Japan Society of Civil Engineers estimation. NISA knew that TEPCO had not prepared any measures to lessen or eliminate the risk, but failed to provide specific instructions to remedy the situation.

We found evidence that the regulatory agencies would explicitly ask about the operators' intentions whenever a new regulation was to be implemented. For example, NSC informed the operators that they did not need to consider a possible station blackout (SBO) because the probability was small and other measures were in place. It then asked the operators to write a report that would give the appropriate rationale for why this consideration was unnecessary. . . .

The regulators also had a negative attitude toward the importation of new advances in knowledge and technology from overseas. If NISA had passed on to TEPCO measures that were included in . . . the U.S. security order that followed the 9/11 [2001] terrorist action, and if TEPCO had put the measures in place, the accident may have been preventable.

There were many opportunities for taking preventive measures prior to March 11. The accident occurred because TEPCO did not take these measures, and NISA and the Nuclear Safety Commission (NSC) went along. They either intentionally postponed putting safety measures in place, or made decisions based on their organization's self-interest, and not in the interest of public safety.

Both Natural Disasters Caused Damage

Although the two natural disasters—the earthquake and subsequent tsunami—were the direct causes of the accident, there are various points in the unfolding of the event that remain unresolved. The main reason for this is that almost all the equipment directly related to the

accident is inside the reactor containers, which are inaccessible and will remain so for many years. A complete examination and full analysis are impossible at this time.

TEPCO was quick, however, to assign the accident cause to the tsunami, and state that the earthquake was not responsible for damage to equipment necessary for safety. . . . However, it is impossible to limit the direct cause of the accident to the tsunami without substantive evidence. . . .

Through our investigation, we have verified that the people involved were aware of the risk from both earthquakes and tsunami. Further, the damage to Unit 1 was caused not only by the tsunami but also by the earthquake, a conclusion made after considering the facts. . . .

Additionally, there were two causes for the loss of external power, both earthquake-related: there was no diversity or independence in the earthquake-resistant external power systems, and the Shin-Fukushima transformer station was not earthquake resistant. . . .

Evaluating Operational Problems

There were many problems with on-site operations during the accident. Events make it clear that if there are no response measures for a severe accident in place, the steps that can be taken on-site in the event of a station blackout are very limited. Recovery work . . . should have been conducted swiftly because of the loss of DC [direct current] power, but was not. TEPCO did not plan measures for the IC [isolation condenser] operation, and had no manual or training regimens, so these are clearly organizational problems. Regarding the vent line composition, conducting line configuration work in a situation with no power and soaring radiation levels must have been extremely difficult and time consuming. On top of this, sections in the diagrams of the severe accident instruction manual were missing. Workers not only had to work using this flawed manual, but they were pressed

Photo on previous page: Workers continue repairs on the fourth reactor of the damaged Fukushima Daiichi power plant in July 2012. (© **The Asahi Shimbun/Getty Images.**)

for time, and working in the dark with flashlights as their only light source. . . .

Many layers of security were breached simultaneously, and the power to four reactors was lost at the same time. Had there not been some coincidental events . . . Units 2 and 3 would have been in an even more precarious situation. We have concluded that—given the deficiencies in training and preparation—once the total station blackout occurred, including the loss of a direct power source, it was impossible to change the course of events.

The Emergency Response Was Ineffective

The government, the regulators, TEPCO management, and the Kantei [prime minister's office] lacked the preparation and the mindset to efficiently operate an emergency response to an accident of this scope. None, therefore, were effective in preventing or limiting the consequential damage.

NISA was expected to play the lead role as designated in the Act on Special Measures Concerning Nuclear Emergency Preparedness, which was enacted after a criticality accident at the JCO uranium conversion facility at Tokaimura, Ibaraki Prefecture in 1999. However, NISA was unprepared for a disaster of this scale, and failed in its function.

In the critical period just after the accident, the Kantei did not promptly declare a state of emergency. The regional nuclear emergency response team was meant to be the contact between the Kantei and the operator, responsible for keeping the Kantei informed about the situation on the ground. Instead, the Kantei contacted TEPCO headquarters and the Fukushima site directly, and disrupted the planned chain of command. A TEPCO-Kantei response team was created in TEPCO headquarters on March 15, but this body had no legal authority.

The Kantei, the regulators and TEPCO all understood the need to vent Unit 1. TEPCO had been reporting to NISA, as was the standard protocol, that it was in the process of venting. But there is no confirmation that the venting decision was conveyed to senior members of METI, or to the Kantei. This failure of NISA's function and the scarcity of information at TEPCO headquarters resulted in the Kantei losing faith in TEPCO.

> This unprecedented direct intervention by the Kantei diverted the attention and time of the on-site operational staff and confused the line of command.

The Prime Minister made his way to the site to direct the workers who were dealing with the damaged core. This unprecedented direct intervention by the Kantei diverted the attention and time of the on-site operational staff and confused the line of command. While TEPCO headquarters was supposed to provide support to the plant, in reality it became subordinate to the Kantei, and ended up simply relaying the Kantei's intentions. This was a result of TEPCO's mindset, which included a reluctance to take responsibility. . . .

At the same time, it is hard to conclude that it was the Prime Minister who discouraged the idea of a full pullout by TEPCO, as has been reported elsewhere, for a number of reasons: 1) There is no evidence that the TEPCO management at the plant had even thought of a complete withdrawal; 2) There is no trace of a decision on a complete withdrawal being made at TEPCO headquarters; 3) The evacuation planned before [TEPCO president Masataka] Shimizu's visit to the Kantei included keeping emergency response members at the plant (though evacuation criteria were discussed); 4) The director-general of NISA reported that when Shimizu called him, he was not asked for advice on a full withdrawal; and 5) The off-site center, which was connected through a video conference system, claimed there was no discussion of a complete withdrawal. Crisis management related to public safety should be assured without having to rely on the capability and judgment of the prime minister of any given time.

Evacuation Issues Impacted Public Health and Welfare

The central government was not only slow in informing municipal governments about the nuclear power plant accident, but also failed to convey the severity of the accident. Similarly, the speed of information in the evacuation areas varied significantly depending on the distance from the plant. Specifically, only 20 percent of the residents of the town hosting the plant knew about the accident when evacuation from the 3km zone was ordered at 21:23 on the evening of March 11. Most residents within 10km of the plant learned about the accident when the evacuation order was issued at 5:44 on March 12, more than 12 hours after the Article 15 notification—but received no further explanation of the accident or evacuation directions. Many residents had to flee with only the barest necessities and were forced to move multiple times or to areas with high radiation levels. There was great confusion over the evacuation, caused by prolonged shelter-in-place orders and voluntary evacuation orders. Some residents were evacuated to high dosage areas because radiation monitoring information was not provided. Some people evacuated to areas with high levels of radiation and were then neglected, receiving no further evacuation orders until April.

The Commission has verified that there was a lag in upgrading nuclear emergency preparedness and complex disaster countermeasures, and attributes this to regulators' negative attitudes toward revising and improving existing emergency plans.

Approximately 150,000 people were evacuated in response to the accident. An estimated 167 workers were exposed to more than 100 millisieverts of radiation while dealing with the accident. It is estimated that as much as

1,800 square kilometers of land in Fukushima Prefecture has now been contaminated by a cumulative radiation dose of 5 millisieverts or higher per year. Insufficient evacuation planning led to many residents receiving unnecessary radiation exposure. Others were forced to move multiple times, resulting in increased stress and health risks—including deaths among seriously ill patients. . . .

> "Insufficient evacuation planning led to many residents receiving unnecessary radiation exposure."

While exposure levels are set as a threshold against acute radiation disorder, there is no widely accepted threshold for long-term radiation damage caused by low doses. The international consensus, however, is that the risk does increase in proportion to the dose. The impact of radiation on health may vary from one person to another depending on age, sensitivity to radiation and other factors, some unknown. After the accident, the government unilaterally announced a benchmark on dosage without giving the specific information that residents needed, including answers to questions like: What is a tolerable level of exposure in light of long-term health effects? How do health implications differ for individuals? How can people protect themselves from radioactive substances?

The government has not seriously undertaken programs to help people understand the situation well enough to make their own behavioral judgments. They failed to explain, for example, the risks of radiation exposure to different segments of the population, such as infants and youths, expecting mothers, or people particularly susceptible to the effects of radiation.

A Need for Regulation Reform

The regulators did not monitor or supervise nuclear safety. The lack of expertise resulted in "regulatory capture," and the postponement of the implementation of relevant regulations. They avoided their direct responsibilities by letting operators apply regulations on a voluntary basis. Their independence from the political arena, the ministries promoting nuclear energy, and the operators was a mockery. They were incapable, and lacked the expertise and the commitment to assure the safety of nuclear power. Moreover, the organization lacked transparency. . . .

If the risk factors of tsunami are raised, for example, TEPCO would only look at the risk to their own operations, and whether it would result in a suspension of existing reactors or weaken their stance in potential lawsuits. They ignored the potential risk to the public health and welfare. . . .

Problems with TEPCO's management style, based on the government taking final responsibility, became explicit during the accident. It prioritized the Kantei's intent over that of the technical engineers at the site. TEPCO's behavior was consistently unclear, and the misunderstanding over the "complete withdrawal" from the plant is a good example of the confusion that arose from their behavior. . . .

After the accident, TEPCO continued to avoid transparency in disclosing information. It limited disclosure to confirmed facts, and failed to disclose information that it felt was uncertain or inconvenient. Some examples of continuing disclosure issues include the delay in releasing electricity demand projections used as the basis for rolling blackouts, and the lack in up-to-date information on the core conditions at the plant.

Laws and regulations related to nuclear energy have only been revised as stopgap measures, based on actual accidents. They have not been seriously and comprehensively reviewed in line with the accident response and safeguarding measures of an international standard. As a result, predictable risks have not been addressed.

The existing regulations primarily are biased toward the promotion of a nuclear energy policy, and not to public safety, health and welfare. The unambiguous responsibility that operators should bear for a nuclear disaster was not specified. There was also no clear guidance about the responsibilities of the related parties in the case of an emergency. The defense-in-depth concept used in other countries has still not been fully considered.

Finding the Root Causes

The Commission believes the root causes of this accident cannot be resolved and that the people's confidence cannot be recovered as long as this "manmade disaster" is seen as the result of error by a specific individual. The underlying issue is the social structure that results in "regulatory capture," and the organizational, institutional, and legal framework that allows individuals to justify their own actions, hide them when inconvenient, and leave no records in order to avoid responsibility. Across the board, the Commission found ignorance and arrogance unforgivable for anyone or any organization that deals with nuclear power. We found a disregard for global trends and a disregard for public safety. We found a habit of adherence to conditions based on conventional procedures and prior practices, with a priority on avoiding risk to the organization. We found an organization-driven mindset that prioritized benefits to the organization at the expense of the public.

> Across the board, the Commission found ignorance and arrogance unforgivable for anyone or any organization that deals with nuclear power.

The Kan Government's Initial Disaster Response Was Reasonably Good

Jeff Kingston

In the following viewpoint, a professor at a Japanese university contends that contrary to what many people believe about Japanese prime minister Naoto Kan's response to the 2011 crisis, he did not do such a bad job. His government's initial disaster response was much better than the one to the Kobe earthquake sixteen years earlier, the author maintains. No government could have done a better job of tsunami disaster relief and recovery given the magnitude of the disaster, he asserts. Many of the complaints about the government's response stem from the nuclear accident at the Fukushima nuclear power plant. Although the government's response to the accident might have been better, and it should have kept the people more informed about developments, the

SOURCE. Jeff Kingston, "3/11: Earthquake, Tsunami, and Nuclear Crisis," from *Contemporary Japan: History, Politics, and Social Change Since the 1980s*. Oxford, UK: Wiley-Blackwell, 2013, pp. 198–203. Copyright © 2013 by Wiley-Blackwell. Reproduced with permission of Blackwell Publishing Ltd.

author believes most of the blame for the nuclear crisis falls on the Tokyo Electric Power Company, not the government. Jeff Kingston is a historian, author, and professor of history and director of Asian Studies at Temple University, Japan.

A t 2:46 P.M. on March 11, 2011 a massive 9 magnitude earthquake struck off the coast of Tohoku, the remote northeastern region of Japan. This is the largest earthquake ever recorded in Japan and the fourth largest in the world, one that carried 500 times the destructive power of the magnitude 7 quake that devastated Haiti in 2010. The shaking lasted six minutes and triggered a tsunami that decimated a 500-km stretch of saw-toothed coastline where fishing ports and oyster hamlets were nestled in narrow inlets. The tsunami reached as high as 38 meters in some places. The swathe of destruction spread 5 km inland, destroying 120,000 buildings and 90 percent of the region's fishing fleet. A further 220,000 houses were damaged and 580,000 people were initially displaced due to the devastation. Around 20,000 people died. The entire island of Honshu shifted 2.4 meters to the east while much of the coast is now prone to flooding because of extensive land subsidence. It will take years to restore the extensive areas of farmland submerged in saltwater, let alone rebuild. The overall damages are estimated at some US$300 billion and reconstruction of towns and infrastructure is expected to take a decade. Much can never be replaced.

The Tsunami Inflicted Wreckage and Devastation

The scenes of wreckage and desolation were and remain horrific. Entire communities were wiped off the map, leaving behind piles of waterlogged rubble and debris, and traumatized survivors. Houses, sheered off from

> *This was the most devastating natural disaster ever to hit Japan.*

their foundations, surfed inland on the sea of debris while muddy clothing dangled from the tops of trees and embankments, smashed cars piled on top of one another caked in mud while others teetered on top of four-storey rooftops perched above ruined buildings. Fishing boats were ripped from their moorings and left marooned far inland, surrounded by the remnants of town centers while here and there a concrete structure poked out from a flattened landscape. The sea walls that were supposed to provide protection from tsunami lay in ruins, and port areas were obliterated. Twisted rail lines jutted off collapsed embankments and everywhere the choking dust swirled around endless piles of debris carrying asbestos and the stench of death.

The tsunami also destroyed oil storage facilities and burning oil carried inland by the waves sparked fires in whatever had not been swept away, leaving scorched ruins. A cascade of mud followed rivers far inland, blasting away residential communities and scattering household contents across the flood plains. It was like a war zone, but worse.

This was the most devastating natural disaster ever to hit Japan, an archipelago that is often battered by tremblers [earthquakes], and typhoons and the country that invented the word "tsunami." Seeing the obliterated villages, it is amazing that the death toll was not much higher, a testimony to disaster preparedness and the value of evacuation drills; people knew where to go and many had emergency supplies at hand. It was also lucky that the tsunami hit when schools were in session, as many had recently practiced an evacuation, facilitating an orderly exodus to higher ground. If the tsunami had hit at night, it is certain that the death toll would have been higher. . . .

Photo on following page: Disaster response troops mobilized by the Japanese prime minister search for victims on March 15, 2011, in the Miyagi Prefecture. (© Paula Bronstein/Getty Images.)

A Trigger for a Nuclear Crisis

The blackout caused by the earthquake meant that tsunami-warning sirens did not function, so some people who heard the initial radio broadcasts that greatly underestimated the size of the tsunami did not flee, feeling safe behind their sea walls. The blackout also triggered the nuclear crisis at Fukushima Daiichi nuclear power plant, causing the cooling systems for the reactors and the spent fuel-rod pools to shut down. Backup generators also failed, resulting in meltdowns in three of the reactors within the first 80 hours. Hydrogen gas accumulated in these three containment buildings, causing explosions that ripped apart the structures and releasing radioactive substances over wide areas of Fukushima and neighboring prefectures. The ghastly pall of Fukushima lingers, sparking fears about radiation contamination well beyond the 20-km evacuation zone around the nuclear accident site. But certainly these concerns are highest within the prefecture, as parents wonder if it is safe to let their children play outside or in playgrounds with elevated radiation readings while farmers and fishermen wonder if they will ever be able to resume their livelihoods. People understand that Fukushima was an accident triggered by nature, but also that it was compounded by hubris, human error, and a botched response by TEPCO [Tokyo Electric Power Company] and the government. Battered by the tsunami and fearful of the radiation spewing from Fukushima, the people of Tohoku looked to the central government for hope and help, but discovered that the politics of disaster trumped coming to their aid.

Examining the Prime Minister's Crisis Response

While many people blame Prime Minister Naoto Kan for an inadequate crisis response, compared to other leaders around the world he did not do such a bad job, given that he faced such a complex and cascading catastrophe. The government's initial response was reasonably good and, overall, Kan probably deserves more credit than most observers are willing to give him. Under the dire circumstances of an unprecedented earthquake, tsunami, and nuclear crisis, Kan managed the initial relief operations reasonably well. Having witnessed the bungling response to the 1995 Kobe earthquake, I am impressed by how much better the Kan government's initial disaster response was, although follow-up has been slow because disaster-hit areas have been held hostage to party politics.

> Prime Minister [Naoto] Kan immediately mobilized 100,000 troops and accepted international offers of assistance.

Prime Minister Kan immediately mobilized 100,000 troops and accepted international offers of assistance, which was in stark contrast to the fumbling response to the 1995 Kobe disaster by the LDP [Liberal Democratic Party]-dominated coalition government. Tsunami disaster relief was reasonably fast and effective and evacuees received basic needs. Certainly they had reasons to be frustrated with the pace of relief and recovery, but it is hard to imagine any government performing better given the devastation of ports and other infrastructure in a remote region and the sheer scale of the disaster.

The Fukushima Catastrophe

Much of the public dissatisfaction expressed by citizens outside Tohoku stems from the Fukushima nuclear accident. TEPCO bears primary responsibility for this catastrophe, along with METI [Ministry of Economy, Trade, and Industry] and NISA [Nuclear and Industrial Safety Agency], for failing to properly monitor the nuclear industry, a pattern established under LDP rule. A panel investigating the management of the nuclear crisis does

A Profile of Naoto Kan

Naoto Kan was born in Ube City, Yamaguchi Prefecture, on October 10, 1946. At the age of twenty-four, he graduated from the Tokyo Institute of Technology. The year after, he became a licensed patent agent/attorney and ran a patent office. He became a civic activist and took part in a number of grassroots movements.

In the mid-1970s, Kan turned his attention to mainstream politics. Between 1976 and 1979 he ran for government office three times—and lost three times. Finally, in 1980, he won a seat in parliament. In 1996, he became a cofounder of the Democratic Party of Japan, of which he served several times as party president. He went on to become minister of health and welfare. In that position he gained national popularity when he exposed the government's role in the spread of blood tainted by HIV.

In September of 2009, Kan became deputy prime minister and in January 2010 finance minister. Five months later he was elected the ninety-fourth prime minister of Japan—the nation's fifth prime minister in three years. Kan's tenure in that role was short-lived. He resigned the office a little more than a year later—forced out of office primarily for failing to demonstrate effective leadership in the aftermath of the 2011 earthquake, tsunami, and nuclear meltdown crises.

criticize poor communication within the premier's office that hampered the government's response, and the government's failure to keep the public informed about developments. However, the panel's interim report, released at the end of 2011, places most of the blame on TEPCO for underestimating the tsunami threat, on its workers for the human error in operating the emergency cooling system, and on the failure to practice evacuation procedures or disseminate accurate information in a timely manner.

The accident also revealed the extent to which Japan's leaders had made an enormous commitment to nuclear power that few wished to re-evaluate. The "nuclear village" of pro-nuclear energy advocates, including utilities, bureaucrats, politicians, journalists, and experts, relentlessly vilified Kan because soon after 3/11 he was vocally critical of TEPCO and began raising questions about the safety of nuclear power and advocating increased reliance on renewable energy. Kan complained early on that TEPCO was not providing reliable information, and that this was why he contacted the US for assistance and information soon after 3/11. Following the explosions and meltdowns (TEPCO only acknowledged the meltdowns in May), on March 15 TEPCO informed Kan that it wanted to withdraw all workers from the Fukushima plant, but he refused to allow this. Later Kan revealed his concerns that if emergency workers abandoned the plant, it might have been necessary to evacuate Tokyo—a nightmare scenario.

Shifting the Blame

TEPCO tried to shift blame onto Kan for the hydrogen explosions that blew apart three of the reactor buildings. The utility said that it had suspended venting of hydrogen that was building up in the buildings due to the overheating of the fuel rods so that Kan, who visited the site by helicopter on March 12, would not be exposed to radiation emitted by the venting. In fact, TEPCO staff had debated the merits of venting throughout the night of March 11, but when they decided to vent [they] realized they had no backup electricity to activate the system. None of the workers had been trained in manually operating the vents, nor could they get to the central control room where manuals were stored, because of dangerous levels of radioactive contamination. Kan had nothing to do with the venting delay and TEPCO belatedly acknowledged this. TEPCO also sought to blame Kan for the suspension of using seawater to cool off the reactors, implicating him in the meltdowns. Kan never issued such an instruction, but apparently the TEPCO liaison in the prime minister's office told the plant operator that the "mood" in the office was opposed to seawater cooling. In the event, the plant manager followed international safety protocols that empower him to make such decisions during an emergency and never did suspend the seawater cooling. Again, TEPCO had to retract its discrediting accusation, but not until the damage to Kan's reputation had been done by a tractable media.

> TEPCO [Tokyo Electric Power Company] also sought to blame Kan for the suspension of using seawater to cool off the reactors, implicating him in the meltdowns.

In the aftermath of the Fukushima disaster, Kan also pressured Chubu Electric into shutting down the Hamaoka nuclear plant because it is sited on an active fault line where seismologists predict there is an 87 percent chance of a mega-quake within the next 30 years. Given the well-known seismic dangers and attendant risk of tsunami, it is amazing that there was no protective seawall. Chubu Electric is constructing an 18-meter high, 1.6-km long seawall costing some US$1.3 billion to protect the plant that is located 200 km from Tokyo, closer than Fukushima Daiichi (240 km). . . .

Kan Revises the National Energy Strategy

Kan became a forceful advocate of renewable energy following the nuclear accident. Ironically, on the morning of March 11, his cabinet had approved legislation outlining a feed-in tariff (FIT) that subsidizes renewable energy sources and creates incentives for expansion of capacity. FITs have played a crucial role in ramping up renewable energy generating capacity in Germany. At the time, the METI-drafted bill envisioned replacing carbon fuels with renewable energy such as solar, wind, and geothermal. In the wake of Fukushima, however, the implications shifted dramatically. Suddenly, the nuclear village saw the FIT as a threat, one heightened by Kan's advocacy for replacing nuclear with renewable energy. In a series of speeches in May 2011 Kan outlined his vision for expanding renewable energy to 20 percent of national electricity generating capacity, sharply up from the existing 1 percent level (9 percent if one includes large-scale hydroelectric projects).

Kan also hit the reset button on the national energy strategy that had been finalized in 2010, scrapping plans for building an additional 14 reactors by 2030 to raise nuclear electricity generating capacity to 53 percent of the total, up from the pre-3/11 level of 29 percent. Further, he called for separating NISA from METI because there was an inherent conflict of interest between the pro-nuclear energy ministry and the nuclear watchdog agency; as of mid-2012, plans to establish a new Nuclear Regulatory Agency within the Environment Ministry remain unrealized. Kan also advocated ending the utilities' monopoly on generating, transmitting, and distributing electricity in order to create opportunities for renewable energy providers. . . . Although Kan had good reasons to target these bureaucratic and utility interests, the nuclear village decided he had gone too far and thus had to go.

The Japanese Government Needs to Revamp Its Disaster Response Plan

Leo Bosner

In the following viewpoint, a veteran employee of the US Federal Emergency Management Agency maintains that there were eleven deficiencies, or shortfalls, in the Japanese government's response to the 2011 natural disasters. One—the most important—is the government's lack of a comprehensive, realistic plan for responding to national disasters. Another is the lack of a uniform incident management system. A third is the failure to fully utilize the potential of nonprofit organizations, volunteers, and donations. Based on the shortfalls, the author offers recommendations to the Japanese government, one of which is that the government put one person in charge of disaster response planning. Leo Bosner is an emergency management specialist who has helped US and Japanese groups and individuals in their efforts to provide disaster relief to Japan and analyze and strengthen Japan's emergency management system.

From January 9 until February 23, 2012, I was in Japan on an invitational fellowship from the Japan Society for the Promotion of Science (JSPS). . . .

Having worked for the U.S. Federal Emergency Management Agency (FEMA) for nearly thirty years, the subject of my fellowship was Japan's response to a large-scale disaster, and whether it could be improved. Under it, I interviewed individuals who were involved in or were familiar with the response to the March 11, 2011 earthquake/tsunami disaster in eastern Japan and lectured on local-level disaster response planning. . . .

> The tragic events of March 11 brought out the very best in the Japanese people's willingness to help others.

In the course of this project, I conducted 28 interviews, gave 20 lectures, and attended two national disaster conferences. I traveled across Japan from Tohoku in the northeast to Kyushu in the southwest and many points in between. I also visited disaster sites in Iwate and Miyagi Prefectures, and spoke with numerous responders who had served on the front line in the disaster.

From everything I saw and heard, the tragic events of March 11 brought out the very best in the Japanese people's willingness to help others. Neighbors rescued neighbors, government agencies mobilized quickly, and volunteers came forward in record numbers. Even today, more than a year later, countless individuals are working to help alleviate the suffering of the disaster survivors.

Three Major Shortfalls in the Disaster Response

But in the course of my visit and interviews, it was impossible to avoid noting numerous shortfalls in the disaster response.

First and foremost, it was clear to me that the Government of Japan simply does not have a comprehensive, realistic plan for responding to large disasters. Rather, the Japan Government's disaster response plan seems to consist of numerous government agency plans that are unrelated to each other. In many cases these plans failed to address or even acknowledge problems that were occurring in the field. In part, this is because the government lacks trained, experienced disaster response professionals. As a result, the government's response to the March 11 disaster was poorly managed and coordinated, and many people suffered needlessly. I was told of numerous problems in this regard, for example:

- Valuable commodities such as food and medicine were often delivered to locations where they were not needed, while survivors at other locations suffered shortages.

- In some cases, much-needed donations were turned away due to the government's inability to receive and manage donations.

- Requests from medical staff in the field for urgently needed help went unanswered.

Second, the Japan Government's lack of effective disaster response planning extends to many Japanese cities and prefectures.

Prefectural and municipal officials in Japan are expected to be the first line of defense in dealing with disasters, but they receive almost no training in disaster response from the Japan Government. Prefectural staff were often described by responders as "doing their best,"

but not being very effective due to their lack of disaster knowledge or training.

Third, the lack of a uniform incident management system added to the confusion and poor use of resources. Large-scale disaster response is a complex endeavor that requires extensive management. Many

In Kesennuma, a particularly hard-hit area, families line up for a meal in an evacuation center. (© Paula Bronstein/Getty Images.)

of the responders I spoke with told of having to invent their own management systems in the midst of the disaster to try to coordinate the activities of multiple jurisdictions that were delivering services to a huge and diverse group of survivors who were themselves widely scattered in shelters across the disaster-stricken area. The responders are to be commended for devising management systems in the midst of disaster, but this is not the best way to run a disaster response.

> Donations of critical items such as food were turned away by the government at the very time when many survivors were desperately in need.

The Impact of Ineffective Donations Management

Fourth, the government did not fully utilize the potential of volunteers, donations, and Non-Profit Organizations (NPOs). The government did not appear to have a plan for incorporating NPOs or donations management into the disaster response. As a result, NPOs received little or no advice from the government as to what was needed or where, and were left to their own devices (and personal connections) to send aid into the disaster area. Donations of critical items such as food were turned away by the government at the very time when many survivors were desperately in need. On the other hand, unneeded donations poured into some areas, resulting in oversupplies of food and medicine in some locales while others faced severe shortages.

Fifth, communication between the government and the field responders seemed to go in one direction only, from the top down. Field responders such as medical doctors, pharmacists, and public health specialists at the disaster sites had no effective means to notify the government of their requirements. Instead, the government appears to have relied in large part on the news media for information regarding the disaster conditions. This result was that the government was often completely unaware and/or misinformed as to what was needed in the field, leading to a misallocation of resources such as food and medicine as cited above.

Sixth, shelter management in the disaster-stricken areas was weak and inconsistent, and in some cases appeared to be nearly nonexistent. Many shelters were described as either being "self-managed" or having "no management." Local residents did their best to manage local shelters in the absence of any government presence or any guidance on shelter management. The result was a very uneven level of management where some shelters [were] very well run and others were not.

Seventh, nutritional needs of the disaster survivors were met very poorly, often consisting only of some rice, bread, and water daily in the early stages following the disasters. This poor nutrition, when combined with the already-weakened condition of many of the survivors, resulted in additional illnesses and medical needs among the survivors that in all likelihood could have been avoided by simple nutritional planning. Some doctors feel that this nutritional deficit may have contributed to fatalities among the survivors, especially the elderly. There did not appear to be any effective plan for meeting the nutritional needs of the disaster survivors.

Developing a Comprehensive Response Plan

Eighth, the government may be overly relying on the Self Defense Force (SDF) for disaster relief. The SDF was quickly mobilized and dispatched in large numbers on March 11 and in the days that followed. This willingness to utilize SDF, and SDF's ability to respond quickly, is an enormous benefit to Japan's disaster response capability. However, it also carries the risk of over-reliance on SDF to the detriment of broader government-wide disaster

JAPANESE OPINION OF GOVERNMENT AND TEPCO EFFORTS, SPRING 2012

	Approve	Disapprove
Government's Overall Efforts from Earthquake and Tsunami	37%	60%
Government's Handling of the Situation at the Fukushima Nuclear Plant	17%	80%
TEPCO's Handling of the Fukushima Crisis	9%	88%

Taken from: PewResearch Global Attitudes Project, "Japanese Wary of Nuclear Energy," June 5, 2012, p. 4. www.pewglobal.org.

response planning. It is also questionable as to whether the SDF itself has sufficient resources to address the full range of disaster response planning in such areas as nutritional planning, shelter management, public health, communications, and others listed in the recommendations below.

Ninth, as a result of the above issues, many individual groups in Japan are now developing their own disaster response plans independent of the Japan Government. Many of the responders and organizations I spoke with are tired of waiting for the government to address their concerns, and are beginning to develop their own independent plans for future disasters. While this is fully understandable given the problems that occurred in last year's disaster response, it would also seem likely that a proliferation of separate and unrelated disaster response plans will add to the confusion in future disasters. On the other hand, if the government can reach out and include these groups in developing a comprehensive response plan, the result could be a greatly strengthened disaster response system.

Tenth, Japan has a wealth of skilled disaster response professionals, but nearly all of this skill lies outside of either the Cabinet Secretariat or the Cabinet Office for Disaster Management, the two Japan Government offices nominally in charge of managing the response to large disasters. Staff who I met from the Cabinet Secretariat and the Cabinet Office for Disaster Management were uniformly bright, dedicated, and hard-working people, but rarely did either they or their leaders appear to have much experience with disasters, and those staff members who gained experience in last year's disaster will soon rotate away to other jobs.

> There does not seem to be any feedback mechanism to use lessons learned from this disaster to improve preparedness for future such events.

One box on the Cabinet Secretariat's organization chart is labeled "Expert Committee for Responses to Situations." In fact, however, it appears to consist not of "experts" but just high-ranking political officials. Most true disaster experts I met were either in the SDF, the fire service, the health and medical professions, or non-profit organizations, but the Japanese Government did not appear to be drawing upon this expertise to strengthen its disaster response plans.

Eleventh, finally, and perhaps most discouraging of all, there does not seem to be any feedback mechanism to use lessons learned from this disaster to improve preparedness for future such events, which unfortunately are likely to occur given Japan's level of risk to disaster.

While the Japanese Government may tinker with some of the details, I neither saw nor heard of any effort to comprehensively address the issues outlined above.

Learning from Experience

Based on my research, I would make seven recommendations to the Japanese Government:

1. Learn from the experience of the disaster responders and experts. During my 46-day visit to Japan under the JSPS Fellowship, I spoke with numerous disaster responders and disaster experts and heard many stories of the successes and failures of the earthquake/tsunami response. However, in the course of 20 lectures and 28 interviews, I cannot recall anyone telling me that the Japanese Government had asked for their opinions or inputs as to how to strengthen the response for future disasters.

> The Japanese Government's disaster response plan seems to consist of numerous government agency plans that are unrelated to each other.

I strongly recommend that the Japanese Government make an intensive effort to reach out to the many disaster responders and experts and learn from them what needs to be done to strengthen Japan's ability to respond effectively to future disasters.

2. Put someone in charge of disaster response planning and the response itself. As it now stands, no one person or agency in the Japanese Government is really in charge of disaster response planning. Responsibility is dispersed among numerous staff and officials who continuously come and go. With no one person in charge of disaster response planning, no one person is credibly in charge of disaster response either, and we are left with the Prime Minister of Japan himself shouting orders into a phone during the disaster. Whatever qualities the Prime

Minister may have, it is unlikely that he will be a professional disaster response manager, nor should he be. The government needs to have a full-time disaster manager (with staff) who is knowledgeable in the field of disaster management and who is empowered to develop a strong national disaster response system.

Developing a National Disaster Plan

3. Move away from hazard-specific planning toward all-hazard planning. The Japanese Government uses "hazard-specific" disaster planning, that is, one plan for an earthquake, another for a tsunami, another for a terrorist incident, and so forth. From my experience, that approach is badly outmoded and leads to confusing and impractical plans as well as numerous gaps in response.

I recommend the "all-hazard" approach, whereby plans are categorized not by type of disaster but by mechanism of the disaster response. . . .

No planning approach is perfect, but the all-hazard approach would go a long way toward ensuring that a full range of disaster-related problems are planned for ahead of time.

4. Develop a comprehensive and realistic national disaster response plan. As noted above, the Japanese Government's disaster response plan seems to consist of numerous government agency plans that are unrelated to each other. In many cases these plans fail badly to address the actual problems that occur in disasters.

For example, one physician in Tohoku told me of his attempts to deal with a serious health problem involving disaster survivors who may have ingested dangerous chemicals from the tsunami waters. But when the physician tried to get help or advice from the government, he learned that three separate offices of the Health Ministry (in Tokyo) had jurisdiction over the problem . . . and that it would be up to him to try to get an answer out of the three separate offices in the midst of his own disaster relief work!

A comprehensive and realistic plan . . . would address the types of problems that occur in disasters and propose realistic solutions.

Implementing a National Incident Management System

5. Implement a national incident management system such as the National Incident Management System (NIMS) that is used in the U.S. "Incident management" sounds like an abstract concept, but it is a very real problem in a disaster. Large-scale disaster response is a complex endeavor that requires extensive management capability. A lack of systematic management can mean, for example, that some stricken towns will be deluged with food supplies while others are neglected. March 11 responders told of having to invent their own management systems in the midst of the disaster to try to coordinate the activities of multiple jurisdictions who were delivering multiple services to a huge and diverse group of survivors who were themselves widely scattered in shelters across the disaster-stricken area. How to prioritize needs? How to ensure that all geographic locations have been reached? How to avoid duplication of effort and misallocation of resources? The middle of a disaster is not the time and place to try to invent a system to address these and other crucial questions. I believe that a nationally-accepted incident management system is badly needed in Japan. . . .

> A nationally-accepted incident management system is badly needed in Japan.

6. Train and professionalize emergency managers at all levels in Japan. Under the current system, many Japanese "emergency managers" have little or no experience or training in emergency management! They are assigned to emergency management offices only temporarily, rotating in and out of their jobs every two years or so. . . .

Given the high risk that Japan faces from earthquakes, tsunamis, volcanoes, and a host of other hazards, it seems to me that Japan needs to build a cadre of trained, experienced emergency managers at the national, prefectural, and municipal levels, as well as in the non-government sectors, to face the next crisis. As noted above, Japan actually has a large body of disaster experts that could provide the leadership and knowledge required to accomplish this goal.

Planning for Voluntary Support

7. Plan for the role of NPOs, volunteers, and donations in disaster response. Voluntary support and donations for disaster survivors can be a major contribution to disaster relief if planned for ahead of time. But if not planned for, then volunteers and donations are instead often seen by government agencies as a burden or a distraction to be turned away, as so often happened in 2011.

In the wake of the March 11 disaster, NPOs received little or no advice from the government as to what was needed or where, and were left to their own devices (and personal connections) to send aid into the disaster area. Donations of critical items such as food were turned away by the government at the very time when many of the survivors were desperately in need. On the other hand, unneeded donations poured into some areas, resulting in oversupplies in some areas while other areas faced shortages.

Instead of turning away these important resources, or using them haphazardly with no plan, I recommend that government agencies at all levels begin now to plan how to incorporate and utilize NPOs, volunteers, and donations more effectively in future disasters. . . .

The March 2011 disaster was a catastrophic event that would challenge even the best-planned response system. But saying that a disaster is catastrophic should not be an excuse to neglect disaster response planning; rather, it should be an incentive to make such planning as realistic and effective as possible to deal with future disasters.

The Impact of Disaster

Bill Emmott

In the following viewpoint, written less than a month after the 2011 earthquake, tsunami, and nuclear crisis devastated Japan, an independent writer and consultant on international affairs maintains it is still too soon to predict the long-term impact of the triple disaster. Based on what has been learned from other natural disasters, the least important thing to be concerned about is the economy, he maintains. The disasters that have befallen Japan are a human tragedy that will have definitive political and psychological consequences, he asserts. Given this, only time will tell how Japan will react. In recent years Japan has been gradually disconnecting itself from the global community. He believes the need to stay focused on internal developments and issues may well lead the Japanese to turn even more inward and become even less concerned with global affairs. Bill Emmott is a British journalist, author, and former editor of *The Economist*.

One of the first phrases foreigners pick up when they live in Japan is *ganbatte kudasai,* because it is so commonly used. Japanese say it in parting,

---

Smoke billows from fires caused by the devastating earthquake that hit the densely-populated city of Kobe, Japan, on January 17, 1995, and resulted in more than 6,000 deaths. (© Kurita Kaku/ Gamma-Rapho/Getty Images.)

at moments when Americans or Brits might say "take care" or "have a good one," but the meaning is different. Translated fairly literally, it means "please endure it."

No one can doubt that the Japanese capacity for endurance, the country's almost spiritual sense of stoicism, has just had its greatest test since wartime defeat and destruction in 1945. Sudden death on the scale seen in March 11's [2011] huge earthquake and tsunami is not something that modern, industrialized, mature societies are used to. Nor are they used to the fear of nuclear meltdown and contamination . . . from the potential catastrophic failure of the Fukushima Daiichi nuclear plant in the zone of destruction.

So all of us should be cautious about jumping to conclusions about the long-term economic, political, and psychological impact of these disasters. What we can do, however, is to use analogous experiences, in Japan and elsewhere, to provide a framework for thinking about this issue, to offer clues as to what might matter most in the coming weeks, months, and even years.

Learning from Natural Disasters

The first, and most fundamental, lesson from other natural disasters is that the economy is the least important thing to worry about. Typically, if economic effects are measured simply by gross domestic product, natural disasters cause a short-term loss in output, thanks to the destruction of offices and factories and the disruption to transport links, but after just a few months they actually act like an economic stimulus package.

> The scale of [the disaster] will be unknowable until the nuclear dangers have either transpired or been brought definitively under control.

This is what happened after Hurricane Katrina in the U.S. in 2005, and it was what happened after Japan's last massively deadly earthquake, the temblor in Kobe in 1995 that killed 6,500 people. Reconstruction spending kicks in quickly, creating jobs, raising incomes, and boosting activity. Insurance pays for some of it, government spending and private investment the rest.

The only real difference in the current Japanese disaster is that the scale of it will be unknowable until the nuclear dangers have either transpired or been brought definitively under control. Admittedly, nuclear-power plants are not insured commercially, but rather by the government and the power companies themselves, so in this case more of the costs will fall on the state.

In the end, this reality about the aftermath of natural disasters should remind us of the limitations of GDP [gross domestic product] as a measure: it tells us what happens to output, to economic activity, but tells us nothing about welfare and happiness.

Paying for Reconstruction

But hasn't the Japanese economy been in a weak state for the past two decades, and isn't its government deep in debt? So how can it afford to pay for this reconstruction? Those are the questions many non-Japanese will be asking.

The answers are that, yes, Japan has performed poorly since the mid-1990s, but that is mainly by comparison with its hyperachievements we all became used to in the 1970s and 1980s. Last year, having been hit hard in 2009 by the global economic crisis, Japan's GDP rebounded strongly, by 3.9 percent. Its longer-term record since 2000 has not been great, but given that—thanks to a low birthrate and negligible immigration—the population has been falling slightly, income per head has fared rather better than the headlines suggest.

Japan's true weaknesses have been debt and deflation. Its gross public debt now amounts to 200 percent of GDP. After moneys owed by one part of government to another are netted off, the figure is still 120 percent, well above the U.S. figure of roughly 80 percent. Yet this is almost all financed domestically, so the government should, at this time of national crisis, face no serious difficulty in borrowing more. It could probably even levy a special reconstruction tax, given that at this moment the Japanese people will be entirely prepared to make sacrifices and share the national burdens.

The only economic doubt worth contemplating concerns deflation, or rather inflation. Prices have been falling in virtually every year since 1997, pulling wages and consumption down with them. The one risk associated with the disaster is that this might change. The crisis will create shortages and has anyway destroyed some productive capacity. Money will be poured in as the reconstruction effort gets underway. With this happening at a time when global energy and food prices are also rising, there must be some risk of deflation turning into inflation in Japan.

Examining the Political and Psychological Consequences

But, as previously stated, these economic questions are not really the most important ones. The most important are the political and psychological consequences, for this is a human tragedy, not an economic one.

Those, too, cannot and should not be predicted with dogmatic certainty. We know that Japan has a very resilient society, accustomed to endurance and always displaying a great sense of solidarity. But we also know that its politics has—since the mid-1990s, really, but certainly in the past five years—been chaotic and dysfunctional. Moreover, we should also note that, since the mid-1990s, popular disillusionment with politicians, with government in general, and with big companies has been increasing.

> We know that Japan has a very resilient society, accustomed to endurance and always displaying a great sense of solidarity.

In politics a fairly new party, the center-left Democratic Party of Japan (DPJ), won a historic victory in August 2009, pushing the Liberal Democratic Party (LDP) out of power for the first time since 1955. But the DPJ has since been a big disappointment, divided and ineffective, and is already on its second prime minister since achieving office, Naoto Kan. Just before the disaster it lost its talented young foreign minister, Seiji Maehara, in a political-funding scandal, and the opposition LDP was plotting to force an early general election by blocking passage of the annual budget through Parliament.

For sure, such political maneuvers will now be put into their true, petty perspective by this human tragedy.

The LDP will want to be seen as a supporter of national unity, and the government will at least have a clear agenda for the next few years, namely that of managing the reconstruction.

Yet where the uncertainty must lie is in the popular view of government. The sense of national unity will be strong. So far, Kan and his government are viewed as having handled the crisis well and—crucially—with honesty. But the nuclear aspect of this disaster could complicate things: there is already a history of cover-ups and mistrust about nuclear safety following accidents during the past 20 years, a mistrust that might well now increase. The DPJ government's aim will be to ensure that that mistrust, and possible recriminations about poor safety procedures, are directed at the Tokyo Electric Power Co., the private operator of the Fukushima plant, and at previous LDP governments.

This won't be easy, however, especially as the government will face a tough choice about what to do with Japan's other aging nuclear reactors. Altogether, nuclear power provides nearly 30 percent of Japan's electricity. So if plants are shut down because of safety fears, that will worsen shortages of power and raise costs for customers; but if they are not shut down, the government risks suffering amid a popular backlash against nuclear energy.

The psychological uncertainties are well illustrated by the question of what sort of backlash there will be. The Japanese will be stoical and willing to make sacrifices. But perceived sacrifices with their lives, in the cause of a quicker reconstruction? That could be a harder call.

So, finally, is the question of whether the Japanese will now react to disaster, as in the 1950s, by reenergizing themselves for entrepreneurialism, by deepening their connections with the world, or whether they might instead become more parochial, more inward-looking, as a result.

The Kobe Earthquake

Early in the morning of January 17, 1995, people in the port city of Kobe on the southern coast of Honshu were awakened by the largest earthquake in Japan in seventy-two years. Known as the Kobe or the Great Hanshin earthquake, its epicenter was just 12.5 miles off the coast of Kobe. The 6.9 magnitude quake, which lasted just twenty seconds, registered 7.3 on the Richter scale. Kobe, home to 1.5 million people, was the hardest hit of the cities in the region. A Kobe resident wrote to a friend:

> At 5:46 A.M., January 17, life as I know it came to an abrupt, shattering end. The apartment I was living in was severely damaged. The roof is gone. Everything that could fall, did. . . . I had felt tremors here before; my house was old and shook easily, but the shaking at 5:46 was like nothing I have ever experienced before. I thought the place was collapsing around me as dirt (from the roofing) cascaded onto my head. The world was filled with a bass roar, and the sound of breaking glass, of roof tiles falling, and the shrieks of rending old wood. It went on forever (I can't believe it was only 20 seconds . . .).

The quake injured forty thousand people—more than one-quarter of them from Kobe—and caused the death of more than six thousand people—close to three-quarters of them from Kobe. It left three hundred thousand people homeless and damaged or destroyed several hundred thousand homes and other buildings. It devastated most of the railways in the region, heavily damaged part of the Hanshin Expressway that linked Kobe and the city of Osaka, and demolished almost all of the wharfs parallel to the shoreline in Kobe. According to the World Bank, the cost of damages for the Kobe earthquake was about $100 billion.

The scale of this disaster, vast and shocking though it is, should not be compared directly with that of 1945: it is more limited, and the rebuilding effort is, say, a five-year one, not a matter of decades. But this disaster also comes at a time when Japan's aging population is already feeling buffeted and even a tad threatened by the rise of China, and when the recent trend had been a gradual disconnection from the world rather than the enthusiastic embrace of globalization.

A shock such as this one could have the effect of turning [the] Japanese even more inward, preoccupied as they will have to be with their internal affairs. Understandable though that would be, let us hope not. The world is better off with an engaged and active Japan.

Too Much Self-Restraint Will Harm Japan's National Interest

Geoffrey Tudor

In the following viewpoint, a writer contends that the Japanese are exercising too much *jishuku*—self-restraint—and impacting recovery from the 2011 disasters. *Jishuku* has made being frugal and cutting back important, he explains. Showiness and celebration have ceased to be desirable. Special events and celebrations have been toned down or canceled entirely. As a result, he contends, the travel, hospitality, entertainment, and leisure industries have been hit especially hard. The low level of domestic tourism, in particular, is a matter of concern. Many think that, instead of practicing so much self-restraint, people should be judiciously spending on goods and services that will help bring economic recovery to the areas where it is most needed. Geoffrey Tudor served more than twenty years as a public relations section chief for Japan Airlines and is a correspondent for *Orient Aviation*.

SOURCE. Geoffrey Tudor, "A Letter from Tokyo: Time to Rally," *Orient Aviation*, June 2011, pp. 28, 30. Copyright © 2011 by Wilson Press HK Ltd. All rights reserved. Reproduced by permission.

In Tokyo, I take my car to a local car wash. The usual top deal is a triple wash at 1,500 yen (US$18.50). They now offer only a single wash at 500 yen, to save electricity, they say. The attendant even suggested that I should wash the car myself, manually. Welcome to *jishuku*.

Life in Tokyo some three months after the devastating [March 11, 2011] Great East Japan Earthquake and tsunami continues to be subdued, although it is starting to brighten up, spiritually and physically. People are going out more and in central districts the lights are back on. However, society is being threatened by an unseen menace—self-restraint, or *jishuku*.

Japan has been hit by a quadruple whammy. In the northeast there was the earthquake, the tsunami, the nuclear accident and, as a result, electric power outages and the subsequent impact on industry, commerce and lifestyle. It is the power problem that is affecting life in the capital.

Jishuku takes many forms, but typically involves cutting back on entertaining, less wining and dining, event cancellations and postponing pleasure travel. Any show of ostentation or celebration is considered bad form. Frugality is the way to go.

The Negative Effect of Exercising *Jishuku*

With at least 25,000 dead or missing in the Tohoku region plus the tens of thousands of people left homeless, there has been a considerable debate about the exercising of self-restraint—*jishuku*—in people's daily lives as an expression of respect and sympathy for the victims.

All in all this means that many of the businesses most affected by *jishuku* are in the hospitality and leisure sectors, such as hotels, restaurants, travel agents and airlines. Once the *jishuku* ball starts rolling it's hard to stop.

Peer pressure and group mentality often persuade people to cut back, when they really don't want or need to. For airlines and travel agents, the J-word is bad news indeed.

A recent survey by Taikoku Databank, a private research firm, showed that 66 companies have gone bankrupt as a result of the Great East Japan Earthquake. Of these companies 26 were firms in the sectors vulnerable to people refraining from spending—such as hotels, inns, restaurants and travel agencies.

> "A recent survey by Taikoku Databank, a private research firm, showed that 66 companies have gone bankrupt as a result of the Great East Japan Earthquake."

One major Japanese seasonal ritual that was badly impacted by *jishuku* was the cherry blossom season, which usually runs from late March to early April. Tokyo's major parks are usually open in the evenings and the blossoming trees are floodlit as revellers enjoy their drinking and singing picnics.

This year the lights were turned off and people went home early and sober. Events in local cities in the area were also cancelled. The Emperor called off the annual Imperial Cherry Blossom party—and when the Emperor acts, loyal subjects follow.

Jishuku's Impact on the Japanese Travel Industry

Recently, the Japanese travel industry, already battered by Mother Nature and the fall in customer demand since March 11, suffered a further pummelling in the annual Golden Week vacation period, which this year ran from April 29 to May 9.

On a year-on-year basis, All Nippon Airways (ANA) 2011 Golden Week traffic was down 2.6% on its domestic routes, but up 16.5 % on international routes, thanks to Japan Airlines (JAL) downsizing—plus of course ANA's expansion plans.

Recently emerging from bankruptcy, JAL recorded falls of 24.6% and 31.3% respectively, reflecting the big cuts the carrier has made in capacity as the company restructures.

Japan Rail reported a record 11% year-on-year decline in passengers over the public holiday period, to 9.1 million. East Japan Railway, centred on the huge Tokyo market, announced a 27% decline in passenger numbers.

Travel agency giant, Japan Travel Bureau, estimated that domestic travel in Golden Week fell by 28% year-on-year.

A glimmer of hope was provided by the final results for Japan's two leading carriers. They were better than originally forecast. "Many bookings came in at the very last minute," said ANA spokesperson, Megumi Tezuka. It appeared that some customers decided they had restrained themselves enough.

> In April [2011] a survey by the *Nihon Keizai* newspaper [reported that] nearly 80% of respondents thought the current wave of restraint was excessive.

ANA and JAL feel the effects of *jishuku* could linger for some time and have come up with stimulus fare packages.

ANA is offering weekend discounts from May 14 to June 26 applicable on all domestic routes ranging from 18%–67% lower than regular fares.

JAL has launched "Tokubin" advance purchase domestic fares with cuts in May and June of up to 61%. Japan's original low-cost carrier, Skymark Airlines, has joined in with a "Happy Sunday Campaign" offering all seats on all routes for a flat 10,000 yen (US$124) on June 19, 26 and July 3.

Jishuku Involves Sacrifice

The debate on *jishuku* has focused on whether it actually helps recovery. In April a survey by the *Nihon Keizai* newspaper [reported that] nearly 80% of respondents

thought the current wave of restraint was excessive. Instead, people should be spending on goods and services that bring economic recovery to the stricken areas, such as buying local products and staying at local inns and hotels in tourist areas unscathed by the disaster. In other words, spend, but spend sensibly so that it helps the quake victims.

Mayors of stricken townships have been asking people to visit them to see the devastation, learn from it, prepare from it—and spend some money.

Many prefectures maintain showrooms and shops in Tokyo where they sell local products and promote their

Billboards, shops, and businesses are dark in the fashionable Ginza district of Tokyo on April 9, 2011. (© **Yoshikazu Tsuno/AFP/Getty Images.**)

attractions. Sales at the Fukushima shop near Tokyo's main railway station were up 10-fold last month.

Jishuku involves sacrifice. There's a nationwide campaign in progress to save electricity and most of the neon lights in the Ginza [the major shopping and entertainment district of Tokyo] were turned off in March and April. Railway and subway stations appear gloomy as the lighting is turned down. Many station escalators and elevators are switched off. On some surface trains, the lights are dimmed.

Shops and stores display darkened interiors, but have posters on the entrances saying: "We're open—please excuse the poor light".

Previous estimates of electric power shortfalls this summer have been lowered, as the Tokyo Electric Power Company (TEPCO) has been able to obtain extra capacity, or so we understand. There is still the prospect of a sweltering summer without enough energy to keep air-conditioners operating. Some sacrifices may still be necessary. So *jishuku*, in some form, may still be with us.

In Tokyo, there are no problems with supplies of gasoline, mineral water or toilet paper, as there were in early post-quake days. But up to last month there were shortages of humble 1.5-volt batteries for flashlights as everybody had been buying these up in case of power cuts. If you could find any batteries, you were limited to one pack of two units. On one day I visited six hardware stores before I found a supply.

Jishuku Will Not Help Japan's Recovery

ANA's president, Shinichiro Ito, talking to the *Nihon Keizai* newspaper, expressed his concern about the future.

Although domestically business traffic is at last year's levels, domestic tourism is still in the doldrums, because of self-restraint *(jishuku)* among consumers, he said. "If the situation stays as it is, personal consumption, a key growth driver, will remain stagnant."

Japan has long been a popular tourism destination, but the March 11 disaster destroyed the intangible value Japan has built up over many years "in the blink of an eye", said the ANA president.

He feels it is most important to convey accurate information overseas. Ito pointed out that when the nuclear plant accident surfaced, there was a shortage of information about safety. This resulted in many foreign carriers changing flights from Narita [Tokyo's airport] to Seoul's Incheon International Airport [in South Korea] because of possible radiation fears.

Many international conferences and events, scheduled to be held in Japan, were cancelled or moved elsewhere. Ito believes the disaster could trigger a battle between Asian cities for events and passenger traffic.

If Japan is slow to re-enter this battle, Ito said, "it will harm the national interest".

He's right. *Jishuku* is not the way.

Japan's Meltdown

Emily Parker

In the following viewpoint, a former US government staffer contends that opportunities will arise from the crises brought on by the 2011 disasters. She points to Japan's history and to the belief of many that crises are good in the long run as they stimulate the country to renew itself. A number of possibilities exist to bring about future change, she maintains. For one, the nuclear accident might inspire more spirited public debates about energy policy. For another, the need for large-scale construction might force Japanese industry to become more productive and more willing to open its doors to more foreign labor. Japanese youth, she declares, will have a chance to build a future that looks nothing like the past. Emily Parker is digital diplomacy advisor and senior fellow at the New America Foundation, a former member of the State Department's policy planning staff, and a writer for a number of periodicals, including the *New York Times*.

As Japan picks up the pieces from its earthquake, tsunami, and nuclear crises, the cold, hard numbers are rolling in. A recent *Barron's* article reported that industrial production dropped around fifteen percent in March [2011] from February, and the economy lost more than three million jobs that same month. Retail sales dropped almost eight percent. *Barron's* predicted further drops in production and industrial output, and pointed out that future growth should not be mistaken for prosperity. Millions could remain jobless and homeless, the article warned, government debt sky-high, and consumer goods in short supply. The article concluded that "there is no silver lining to this cloud."

> " Despite these grim numbers there is something, dare we say it, that sounds like hope.

And yet, despite these grim numbers there is something, dare we say it, that sounds like hope. In both Japan and abroad, people are asking: Is this it? Will this be the twenty-first-century crisis that gets Japan back on its feet? These questions are so prevalent in the current discourse that it is worth examining the assumptions behind them. Why do people imagine that the recent horrors will somehow revive Japan, rather than knock it out once and for all? To be sure, some are just repeating the well-worn trope about crisis breeding opportunity, an idea that is hardly particular to Japan. There is also a sense of eagerness, particularly in the Western media, for a new Japanese narrative that evokes vitality rather than stagnancy.

And of course there is Japan's own history, throughout which exogenous shocks have sparked dramatic renewal. Think back to 1853, when Commodore Matthew Perry arrived with his "black ships" and demanded that the closed-off feudal state open its doors to trade. The Japanese rose to the challenge. In the Meiji Restoration that began in 1868, young samurai took power and overhauled the nation in a few short decades. In *Japan Rising,* the historian Kenneth Pyle describes the Meiji leaders as

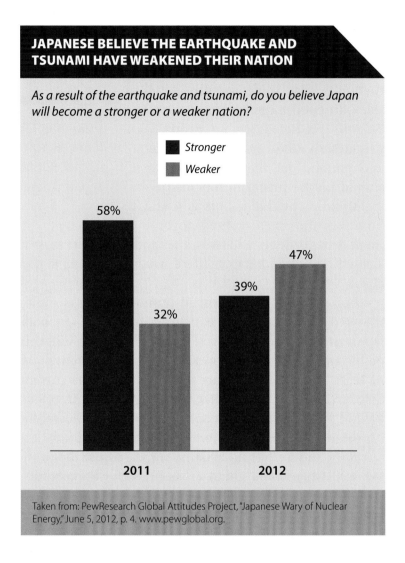

JAPANESE BELIEVE THE EARTHQUAKE AND TSUNAMI HAVE WEAKENED THEIR NATION

As a result of the earthquake and tsunami, do you believe Japan will become a stronger or a weaker nation?

■ Stronger
▩ Weaker

58%

32%

39%

47%

2011   2012

Taken from: PewResearch Global Attitudes Project, "Japanese Wary of Nuclear Energy," June 5, 2012, p. 4. www.pewglobal.org.

being tired of Japan's economic backwardness and sense of inferiority to the West. They were thus ready and willing to sacrifice time-honored institutions to achieve their goals. The Meiji leaders adopted European legal codes, imported thousands of advisers, and built the most centralized state in Japanese history.

An even more well-known example of rebirth is the economic miracle that rose from the wreckage of Japan's World War II defeat. John Dower's *Embracing Defeat* describes the crushing years that followed the war: "Despair took root and flourished in such a milieu; so did cynicism and opportunism—as well as marvelous expressions of resilience, creativity, and idealism of a sort possible only among people who have seen an old world destroyed and are being forced to imagine a new one."

There is also a general impression of the Japanese as remarkably hard-working and resilient, and even this cliché contains a few grains of truth. Look at the Japanese language, for example. This is a country where people don't say "good luck," but rather *ganbatte,* which roughly translates as "try your best." Where we in America say "I'm sorry," the Japanese say *moshiwake arimasen,* which is closer to "there's no excuse." Recent stories about the dignity, civility, and stoicism of ordinary Japanese only reinforce this image of a people that respond bravely to crisis.

I have some personal experience with the indefatigable Japanese spirit, thanks to two years of training in a martial-arts dojo in Kyoto. We ran barefoot through the city streets, were thrown down on wooden floors, and wore short-sleeved cotton uniforms throughout the bone-cold winter. As our skills increased, so did the dojo master's expectations: with a higher belt came public humiliations and harsher scoldings. There were no excuses. And so we all demonstrated *gaman,* endurance, through the physical pain and the cold and the tongue-lashings. As a result, our progress, both individually and as a dojo, was extraordinary.

The Japanese have been known to respond boldly to hardship, which may be why in recent years various people in Japan have suggested to me that the country needed a greater "sense of crisis." The bursting of the Japanese bubble in the early 1990s and the

> The bursting of the Japanese bubble in the early 1990s and the lost decade that followed were dramatic, but they didn't leave the nation in tatters.

lost decade that followed were dramatic, but they didn't leave the nation in tatters. Early on, decisionmakers tried to stem panic: banks weren't allowed to fail; bad loans were swept under the rug. Some economists later said that if Japan had allowed itself a harder fall, a short period of intense suffering might have prevented years of lost growth.

We may never know for sure. What we do know is that even after the bubble burst, a visitor to Tokyo might be struck by all the well-dressed girls in Tokyo, gossiping with their friends over coffee and cake. Cities were clean and efficient, people polite. Those brown leather handbags were ubiquitous. A kind of "Louis Vuitton recession."

Occasionally the Western media would decide that Japan was back, and would wax poetic about the "lion-haired" Prime Minister Junichiro Koizumi, with his post office reform and attempts to crush the "dinosaurs" in his own Liberal Democratic Party. And yet, if you visited Japan during those periods you did not get the sense of a country on the move. I would constantly hear sentiments along the lines of *kibo ga nai*—there's no hope.

From a distance, Japan still looked slick and shiny, with a luxury handbag dangling from one arm. But there were shadows everywhere, and they weren't always visible to the naked eye. Most looming was Japan's rapidly aging society, and the related problems of an impending labor shortage and overburdened pension system. Some of the more obvious responses to this problem, such as opening Japan's doors to foreign labor, seemed culturally abhorrent. There was an almost visceral feeling of impending doom, yet people appeared to be frozen in place, waiting for the curtain to fall. Young people didn't want to get married or have kids, they were deciding to live at home, or even, quite literally, to never leave the house.

Japan's younger generation seemed utterly disinterested in politics, as if there was simply no point. And after Koizumi's star-studded run, a series of Japanese prime ministers rose and fell in rapid succession while the people waited for a true leader to emerge. There was a sense of bleakness—but not necessarily crisis. It was what my dear friend Kazuo Noda would call *hyogen dekinai fuan,* or "inexpressible uneasiness." Noda-san, who had lived through World War II and vividly remembered the agony that followed, referred to the lost decade of the 1990s as "the second defeat." The second defeat was worse than the first, he once told me, because "there was no enemy, we lost to ourselves. When you've lost to yourself, it's very hard to rebuild."

> Now people are starting to ask if—and how—this crisis might somehow, over the long term, revitalize Japan.

While some Japanese may have yearned for a sense of crisis to shake people out of their stupor, nobody would have wished for a human tragedy or the scale of the nuclear disaster. Yet here it is. So now people are starting to ask if—and how—this crisis might somehow, over the long term, revitalize Japan. While it's hard to determine the probability of such an outcome, we can look at the possibilities for future silver linings.

First of all, we may start to see more vigorous public debates about energy policy. A Japanese journalist, who asked not to be named in this [viewpoint], told me that previously people blindly adhered to the government's nuclear policies and their belief in the safety of Japan's nuclear plants. Now there is more soul-searching over the best ways to pursue safe energy, as well as over proper oversight of the power industry. Regardless of what the answer turns out to be, he adds, "It is good for an economy to have a more thinking population, which could lead to more innovations, more unique ideas, more diverse opinions."

There may be other opportunities as well. Paul Sheard, chief economist at Nomura, suggests this crisis

Shoppers browse along the luxury shops of Tokyo's Ginza shopping district in September 2011. The Japanese economy—the third largest in the world—has a history of recovering from deep crises. (© Kiyoshi Ota/Bloomberg/Getty Images.)

could offer an opportunity for Japan to finally emerge from the deflationary cycle that has plagued the country since the mid-1990s. Because of capital destruction and the need for reconstruction spending, supply-demand conditions are likely to tighten. Ending deflation, Sheard adds, would also require more aggressive economic stimulus in the form of expansionary fiscal and monetary policies.

Sheard also explained that the need for large-scale construction could force Japan to open its doors to more foreign labor. Yoichi Funabashi, the editor in chief of the *Asahi Shimbun*, told me that there could be other immigration opportunities as well. "We are now witnessing tremendous downward pressure in terms of production and consumption," Funabashi told me. "Once it starts to recover and get into the creative destruction stage, I think the demand for labor will increase. The only way for Japan to revitalize is for it to be more integrated into the global economy. For that to happen, Japan will have to recruit more globally competitive people, even in manufacturing, automobile, and electronics industries."

New uncertainties—about the availability of electricity, for example—could lead manufacturing companies to shift production overseas. While some would argue that Japan should respond by focusing on new industries, others have a different take. "What they need is not so much new industries, but to make old industries more productive," says Richard Katz, editor of the *Oriental Economist Report*. Temple University's Robert Dujarric says that there is certainly room for improvement in services, for instance. "The hospitality industry, retailing, transportation, education, etc., could all become more efficient if the regulatory environment changed," Dujarric says. "For example, JAL and ANA enjoy a de facto duopoly in the airline market."

> After years of subtle disappointment and 'inexpressible uneasiness,' Japan must now decide the kind of country that it wants to be.

Then there is the political question. Now more than ever, Japan needs a strong new leadership, it needs vision, and the people need to be engaged and involved. In a positive scenario, this crisis would put an end to the infighting that has plagued both the Democratic Party of Japan and the Liberal Democratic Party. Then, leaders could focus on the issues that really matter—reconstruction, nuclear safety, social security reform, to name just a few.

Something, clearly, has to give. After years of subtle disappointment and "inexpressible uneasiness," Japan must now decide the kind of country that it wants to be. For too long Japan has been suspended between two paradigms. The era of government-led growth and lifetime employment has drawn to a close, but a new model has yet to set in. Today's young inherited a country whose economic glory days were over. There was reason to fear that many would never be as affluent as their parents, and that the nation had essentially peaked.

Many of these young people are now hoarding their money, scared about their future security in an aging society with a weak social security system. "Their prospects for their future seem to be dark right now," Hiromichi Shirakawa, chief economist at Credit Suisse Japan, says of the country's younger generation. "My undergraduate daughter is more conservative than ourselves. She doesn't buy anything. She knows that the demographic situation will weigh on them, so she's saving." Shirakawa adds that he fears this crisis may lead well-educated Japanese to move overseas.

That would be unfortunate. Japan has enormous potential, talent, and skill. The missing ingredient over the last few years, as trite as it sounds, has been hope. Now there seem to be glimmers of this long-missing sentiment, even if sometimes laced with a deep sense of dismay. You can find strains of national pride, and, for better or for worse, Japan is back on the map.

Opportunities will rise from this wreckage, even if they come at a price that no one would ever want to pay. Japan's youth now have a chance to build a future that looks nothing like the past.

Earthquake, Tsunami, Meltdown—The Triple Disaster's Impact on Japan, Impact on the World

Elizabeth Ferris and Mireya Solis

In the following viewpoint, written two years after Japan's triple disaster, two researchers maintain that the effects of the calamity went far beyond Japan. In Japan itself, they contend, the disaster took a major toll economically, politically, and socially, resulting in fundamental changes and making nuclear energy a key topic of public debate. Globally, it highlighted the high economic costs of disasters taking place in developed countries and prompted some governments to announce plans to phase out of nuclear energy. It also revived interest and desire in investing in disaster risk reduction strategies. Elizabeth Ferris is a senior fellow in foreign policy and codirector of the Brookings-London School of Economics Project on Internal Displacement. Mireya Solis is the Philip Knight Chair in Japan studies and senior fellow at the Brookings Center for Northeast Asian Policy Studies, associate professor at American University, and an expert in Japan's foreign economic policies.

Two years ago today [March 11, 2013], a devastating 9.0 earthquake struck Japan's east coast, followed minutes later by a massive tsunami with 100 foot waves. Japan's legendary investment in earthquake-resistant design meant that only about 100 people died in the earthquake itself although almost 20,000 people lost their lives in the tsunami. The economic destruction of the "Triple Disaster" was massive: 138,000 buildings were destroyed and $360 billion in economic losses were incurred. This was the most expensive disaster in human history. Japanese response to the earthquake and tsunami was rapid, effective, and life-saving. Some 465,000 people were evacuated after the disaster. But it was the meltdowns at the Fukushima nuclear plant—the world's worst global nuclear crisis since Chernobyl in 1986—which caused the most fear and provoked the greatest criticism of the Japanese government's response. . . .

The Impact of the Triple Disaster

The economic, political, and social consequences of the Triple Disaster have changed Japan in fundamental ways. The uprooting of entire communities and the large infrastructural losses produced immediate disruptions in Japan's extensive supply networks. These in turn caused dramatic drops in industrial production that imposed a toll not only on Japan's economy, but also on the many other countries linked through these production net-

works. While Japanese companies creatively restored the supply chains in just a few months, the shutdown of the nuclear reactors has had far more damaging long-term economic consequences. Since 3/11 only two nuclear reactors have restarted operations, and the Japanese government has had to resort to large increases in oil imports to make [up] for the gap in electricity supply. Consequently, since 3/11 Japan has experienced record trade deficits, in the order of $78 billion in 2012.

The social and political aftereffects of 3/11 are also formidable. A large citizen movement calling for the abolition of nuclear power in Japan developed in the aftermath of the Fukushima disaster. The enactment of more exacting safety standards and the development of

Protesters hold a banner at an anti-nuclear rally in Tokyo on March 10, 2013, two years after the earthquake, tsunami, and nuclear disaster. (© **Mark Eite/ Aflo Co. Ltd./Alamy.**)

new patterns of government regulation and monitoring of the nuclear industry have emerged as key topics in the national political debate. On a more positive note, the Triple Disaster also revealed Japan's most valuable asset: the strength of its civil society. The world watched in awe as Japanese citizens who had lost everything immediately sprung to help one another. The dignity, creativity, and orderly response of the Japanese population to this mega disaster is indeed the best measure of Japan's potential. And just as a previous natural disaster, the Kobe earthquake of 1995, helped spur the NGO [nongovernmental organization] movement in Japan, March 11, 2011, has seen the activation of scores of non-profit groups and the consolidation of a culture of volunteerism.

> March 11, 2011, has seen the activation of scores of non-profit groups and the consolidation of a culture of volunteerism.

However, the reconstruction challenges remain daunting for Japan. Hundreds of thousands of people are still displaced, the quality of the nuclear cleanup continues to raise concerns, and the financial cost of rebuilding the Tohoku region is staggering (in its latest stimulus budget, the [Japanese prime minister Shinzo] Abe government slated $18 billion dollars for this purpose). Japan's energy future is also uncertain as the government has yet to issue a long-term strategy that clarifies the role of nuclear power in the country's energy mix.

Learning from the Disaster

The effects of the Japanese disaster went far beyond Japan, of course. It served as a warning that even developed, well-prepared countries are not immune from terrifying disasters. It illustrated the extremely high economic costs of disasters occurring in developed countries and the vulnerabilities that come with urbanization and coastal settlement. It served as a wakeup

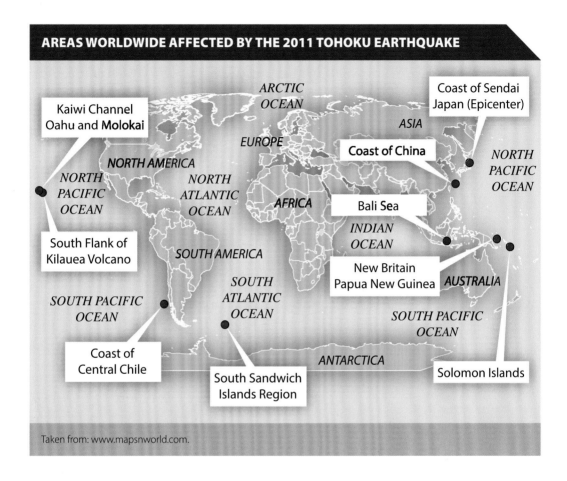

AREAS WORLDWIDE AFFECTED BY THE 2011 TOHOKU EARTHQUAKE

ARCTIC OCEAN

Coast of Sendai Japan (Epicenter)

Kaiwi Channel Oahu and **Molokai**

ASIA

EUROPE

Coast of China

NORTH PACIFIC OCEAN

NORTH AMERICA

NORTH PACIFIC OCEAN

NORTH ATLANTIC OCEAN

AFRICA

Bali Sea

South Flank of Kilauea Volcano

INDIAN OCEAN

SOUTH AMERICA

New Britain Papua New Guinea

AUSTRALIA

SOUTH PACIFIC OCEAN

SOUTH ATLANTIC OCEAN

SOUTH PACIFIC OCEAN

Coast of Central Chile

ANTARCTICA

Solomon Islands

South Sandwich Islands Region

Taken from: www.mapsnworld.com.

call to the world that unanticipated disasters (or "black swans") happen and that those engaged in contingency planning need to be prepared for much more devastating disasters. Internationally, the fallout of the Fukushima meltdowns for the future of nuclear energy has been mixed. While immediately after the accident some governments announced plans to phase out of nuclear energy, others have continued their nuclear planning (although it's probably true that all nuclear plants worldwide looked more seriously at their safeguard mechanisms in light of Fukushima). Japan's tragedy has also led to a re-energizing of investing in disaster risk reduction strategies.

In October 2012, the Japanese government and the World Bank co-hosted the Sendai Dialogue to highlight the lessons learned from the disasters and to adopt comprehensive guidance for reducing risk in other parts of the world. To continue the learning of lessons from Japan for disaster risk management in Asia, we are organizing a day-long conference at Brookings on May 10, 2013 to examine the lessons from March 11, 2011, the challenges of disaster risk management in Asia and, more broadly, strategies for mainstreaming disaster risk management in development assistance. We hope in a small way to contribute to continued learning from Japan's tragedy and to prevent further tragedies resulting from similar disasters which occur elsewhere.

CHAPTER 3

Personal Narratives

A Tokyo Businesswoman Feels Stranded by the Earthquake

Chikirin

Photo on previous page: A rescure worker holds photographs found among the debris left by the tsunami in Sendai, Japan, on March 21, 2011. (© Foto24/Gallo Images/Getty Images.)

In the following viewpoint, a Japanese woman from Tokyo attending a business meeting in Japan's Ibaraki Prefecture the day a 9.0 magnitude earthquake struck on March 11, 2011, recounts what happened and how she and others reacted during the twenty-four hours it took her to get back home. She explains what a loss she was at because she was unfamiliar with the area in which she found herself and expresses her surprise that shops selling food would not accept customers. She paints a vivid picture of what went on at the hotel in whose lobby she slept and of the scene at the various train and bus stations in which she had to wait. She shares her impressions of the people she encountered at each

SOURCE. Tomomi Sasaki, "On Catastrophes and Miracles: A Personal Account," *Global Voices,* March 14, 2011. http://global voicesonline.org/2011/03/14/japan-on-catastrophes-and-miracles-a -personal-account. This article by Tomomi Sasaki was originally published by Global Voices Online, a website that translates and reports on blogs from around the world. Reproduced under CC by 2.5.

place along the way and proclaims how impressed she was with their "miraculous behavior" under such trying circumstances. Chikirin is a full-time blogger and writer.

I was in Ibaraki Prefecture when the earthquake hit. The tremor must have been stronger than in Tokyo. Luckily, I was not hurt. I knew immediately that it was no ordinary earthquake because it was shaking for a long time and the lights went out immediately. The meeting I was attending was promptly dismissed, and we walked down the stairs from the 7th floor to take refuge outside the building.

I was the only one who had come to the meeting from Tokyo, and hence the only one who needed to take a train back to Tokyo. I took a local bus and hurried to the closest station.

Now that I think about it, some cities along the coasts were already engulfed by the tsunami by that time. Not even an hour had passed since the first quake, and people were struggling to make well-informed decisions. I too only knew that the epicenter was in Touhoku, and that it was a very severe earthquake. My mobile phone was dead.

> Only the local buses were functional, but that didn't help me because I didn't know the area very well.

All modes of mass transit at the station were halted and many people were forming lines (meaninglessly so, in retrospect). Only the local buses were functional, but that didn't help me because I didn't know the area very well. I looked for information on how to get back to Tokyo.

There was a vending machine that was still working so I bought some juice and tea. I wanted to get some food too but all the stores had their doors shut. I understood: the cash registers would not have worked because of the power failure, and it is dangerous to have customers in a store during an earthquake. But I thought at least those shops selling food should have accepted customers.

There was a long line for the toilet as well and the water was not running, but people used the facilities with humility. It had somehow become a routine for the person coming out of the toilet to advise the next person not to throw used paper into the toilet.

Finding Lodging

I stayed at the train station for around four hours, until sunset. It was clear that there was nothing to be done. The greatest difficulty for me was the fact that I didn't know anything about the area. I didn't know what kind of hotels, with what kind of capacity the city had, nor what other forms of transport I could find to get home, or how far I could get on foot. Without knowing such things, it was difficult to make appropriate decisions. . . .

When it started getting darker, the people at the station told us that we should look for a place to spend the night, and that they had been advised to say so by the government. People started dispersing. Those who worked nearby went back to their offices.

The only ones left were people who didn't know much about the place and had nowhere to go. I had to find somewhere to stay, it was cold and it was windy. So I asked the station staff for a hotel and headed in that direction. The first hotel I found kindly offered to let me sleep in the lobby because all their rooms were taken. I was wearing a short skirt, so they even provided me with a blanket right after the children got theirs.

Many men who had also sought refuge in the lobby spent the night on chairs without even a blanket. The emergency blanket was made of thickly woven lambs wool and kept us very warm. The entire city had blacked out, but the hotel still had electricity, so some people came to the hotel to recharge the batteries of their mobile phones. (Some people seemed to have no electricity, water or gas at their homes.) . . .

The blanket I had was very big, so I considered taking off my skirt and just wrapping myself up in the blanket. The aftershocks were continuing though, and I thought I probably wouldn't have enough time to slip it back on if we had to flee, so I let that idea go.

There were many people who stayed awake the whole time, but I tried to sleep. I felt chilled because I had been exposed to the wind outdoors for as long as four hours, and I knew I had to gather my strength to get through the situation. I bundled myself and my valuables into the blanket and slept as much as I could.

> I was grateful to the entire staff of the hotel who supported us throughout the night, and the unbelievably well-organised manner in which the evacuees behaved.

Late at night, the hotel staff provided us with a small salted rice ball and a half cup of miso-soup per head. Many people in the lobby waited quietly in lines to receive them. I was grateful to the entire staff of the hotel who supported us throughout the night, and the unbelievably well-organised manner in which the evacuees behaved. Everyone was so quiet.

The hotel let us use some power chargers for our mobile phones, but there weren't enough because there were so many people who wanted to use them. And anyway, the mobile phones were still useless. There was one public telephone in the lobby, so I joined the queue and called home. I got through at 3 A.M. in the morning. When I hung up after telling my family that I was fine, the 100 yen coin that I had dropped in was returned to me. The NTT phone company had made it free to use the public telephone lines.

Time to Move On

In the morning I received one rice ball from the hotel. From the time the earthquake hit [on Friday, March 11, 2011] until 8 P.M. [on Saturday, March 12] when I got back to Ueno [in Tokyo], the only things I'd eaten were two rice balls from the hotel, so I was really thankful to them. Everything was closed including the convenience stores and restaurants around the station, so I wouldn't have been able to eat anything otherwise.

There were aftershocks throughout the night, but I was strangely not afraid. What did scare me was the devastation in Touhoku on the television. I stopped watching after a while. I felt that there were some things that perhaps were better left unseen.

The next morning, I got an update at the station that the trains were unlikely to arrive. However, I was glad to hear that a special bus would go to the closest station from which trains were about to depart. I waited in a long, long line. I passed an extra mask to someone suffering from hay fever. I began to really hate my pumps. I wanted to buy sneakers, but the store wasn't open. . . .

No one went to ask for another rice ball at the hotel even when there were some left. (The hotel staff took the remaining ones, and went to check whether there was anyone on other floors who hadn't eaten yet). In those 24 hours, I don't know how many times I thought, "this country is unreal".

I'm not writing to advertise what a terrible experience I had. What I experienced was not the damage of an earthquake. It was a minor inconvenience that might not even deserve to be described as "confusion", but I wanted to write down what it was like, while I clearly remembered the events.

What I want to communicate is the miraculous behavior of the people of this country. I didn't encounter a single "angry", "shouting" or "complaining" person in the 24 hours. I only saw one drunk middle-aged guy who was having a fit in Ueno station. This country is truly miraculous.

The Journey Home

Everyone was quiet even when waiting at the long queues for the special buses. At some point, the line split into two: one for those who wanted to sit, and another for those who didn't mind standing. This sense of order took me by surprise. . . .

I hesitated for a moment because someone had told me that the bus journey was 1 hour long, but I decided that I didn't need to sit because we couldn't tell when the next bus was going to arrive. The bus drove on roads that were not designed for buses: very narrow and winding. I was exhausted by the time I arrived at the JR station [in Tokyo] seething with people. (Anywhere north of this station continues to be disconnected now, so the damages must be severe.)

The elevator didn't work, so I climbed up the long flight of stairs. The station staff had no answers for the questions people had; when would the train come, or when would the next train depart. Still, all the people waited quietly. They all knew they wouldn't know, and they didn't want to bother someone who had been working tirelessly and sleeplessly.

A train reached the platform. Not surprisingly, it was full of people. Many more people couldn't get home here from Tokyo than the other way around. . . .

At all doors, all passengers were allowed to get off first, and then the people in the queue calmly began to get on board. No one tried to push to get to an empty seat (well, you could say that everyone was exhausted at that point). My feet were bruised due to the bumpy journey on the bus, so I took off my pumps and spent the rest of the journey on bare feet.

By the way, I do think that Twitter and the Internet are useful in a disaster, but in my own experience, I couldn't check the Internet or my mobile phone for the 24 hours from when I decided to go home and the moment I eventually arrived. My only connection to the outside world was the green public telephones and the TV that the hotel made available to us.

Many people along the way had smartphones, tablets, or PCs, but I doubt if any of them had any Internet access. . . .

> Many people along the way had smartphones, tablets, or PCs, but I doubt if any of them had any Internet access.

Arriving at Home

When I got to Ueno station, I knew that the number of people who were stuck in Tokyo were several orders of magnitude greater than those who couldn't get back to Tokyo.

Additionally, the orderly situation in Ueno station was unbelievable. In order to let people into the platform by increments, control cordons was made at the stairs, ticket wickets, and everywhere. The people who [were] stopped there [were] proceeding step by step, following the interaction. Policemen of Tokyo Metropolitan Police Department stood guard. . . .

I was also amazed by the composure of the people who were waiting. Most people had spent one night with little more than the clothes on their back. Everyone was hungry, and had not slept enough, and were distraught. The people who were bound north towards Touhoku must have also been worried about their families. . . .

When leaving the station we were led to the passages that are normally used by the offices so to avoid the gates that were filled with people who were trying to get back to their homes in the provinces. They didn't check our tickets. There were more important things to do than checking whether people had paid for their fare.

JR's operations were fiercely focused on moving the trains as soon as possible. . . .

After that, I got home on the subway. I took off my shoes again because my feet hurt too much. The chocolate I bought in Ueno station was delicious. I thought that I should carry chocolate or candies with me at all times.

When I finally arrived in front of my apartment, I saw a sign on the elevator saying "Inspection required". It brought a resigned smile to my face, and I climb the stairs. It had taken me more than 24 hours to arrive since the moment I decided to go home.

A Foreign Student Experiences the 2011 Earthquake

Sasicha Manupipatpong

In the following viewpoint, a young woman attending an international private day school in Tokyo shares her experiences during the 2011 earthquake. She explains that she was in class only half listening to the teacher and feeling light-headed when she realized that the building was swaying. She shares her thoughts as she followed the last of her classmates out the door to the high school field where they waited to be allowed to go home. She goes on to tell what she did later that night and why she was not sure what to believe about the severity and effects of the earthquake. She relates what she learned personally about being a foreigner in Japan during the crisis. At the time this viewpoint was written, Sasicha Manupipatpong was a student at the American School in Japan.

SOURCE. Sasicha Manupipatpong, "The Earthquake and Me: A Personal Account of the Japan Earthquake," Student News Action Network, March 28, 2011. http://newsaction.tigweb.org. Copyright © 2011 by Sasicha Manupipatpong. All rights reserved. Reproduced by permission.

2:40, Friday. Or at least that's what it was when I last looked at the clock.

As Mr. Chambers switched from explaining to us the difference between acids and bases to regaling us with tales of his childhood adventures, I drifted off into a slight daze, lightheaded from having slept at 3 in the morning every day for the whole week and relieved that there was only 20 minutes left to endure until I could get caught up with my sleep debt. It was only after a voice from the back of the room jolted me awake that I realized my wooziness was not from my sleep deprivation, but rather the swaying of the school building. The whole class sat in silence for a while, waiting the earthquake out, all of us sharing the thought that it would pass like all the previous minor tremors that constantly shook Japan. But, the thing was, the tremors, far from subsiding, increased in amplitude. "You may want to get under the tables now," instructed Mr. Chambers, in a voice no different than that we heard in class every day, albeit more somber, as he looked out the window towards the P.E. class shivering outside in shorts and T-shirts. Still slightly out of it, I got up and crammed myself into the small area under my wooden desk, which, to my disgust, had gum stuck on its underside.

> The whole class sat in silence for a while, waiting the earthquake out, [but] the tremors, far from subsiding, increased in amplitude.

A Confusing Experience

Our class, still remarkably composed, remained under the protection of our desks for what seemed like forever. Meanwhile, I watched the water in the fish tank, murky with all the algae and leaves that were churned up during the shaking, sway from side to side and nearly spill over the side of the aquarium walls. But other than the students that were crouching under their tables, the turbulent swirling of the water in the fish tank, and, of course, the trembling of the ground, there were no indicators that there was an earthquake going on. There was no running, no shouting, and no screaming. It seemed so mundane that I felt less like we were going through a natural disaster and more like one of those earthquake drills we so often had. What fear I felt was all for my parents, for my mom because she was at home alone and probably didn't know what to do in an earthquake, and for my dad because he was in a high rise building and would have to climb down the stairs with his bad leg.

> It seemed so mundane that I felt less like we were going through a natural disaster and more like one of those earthquake drills we so often had

Once the ground stopped with its quaking, my classmates emerged one by one from our desks and headed for the high school field, going off at different paces and directions like sheep in a flock without a herder. I stood stunned for a while, staring at my scattered stationery and notebooks, trying to figure out what to bring out with me, because unlike an earthquake drill, there was a chance that I might not be allowed to get back in to pick up my bag—it felt sort of like one of those extremely surreal and peculiar "what would you bring if you were only allowed to take one thing onto a deserted island with you" type of situations. As the last of my classmates trailed out the door, however, I gave up trying to choose and just snagged my jacket and followed them.

"Run! Run! Run!" Those were the first words I heard when I got out of the building and was making my way through the winding courtyard. Being the stickler about rules that I was, I frowned at the blatant breach in earthquake situation protocol and searched for the person to whom the voice belonged. A teacher. Interesting. In that case, I thought, I guess I'd better start running. And so I ran.

Learning the Magnitude of the Disaster

3:50 on the same day: the next time everything calmed down at the field enough for me to think to look at my watch.

It took about 40 minutes for all the head counting to finish and for the students to finally regain their voices and their typical impatience to remember to begin bombarding the teachers with questions of when they could finally go home. I sat in a tight circle of friends on the fake grass flicking black pebbles at my neighbor's leg and discussing how we already broke 3 out of 4 of the earthquake protocol rules that Japanese schools taught their students in elementary school when another wave of students got up to go and the teachers began shouting that nobody was allowed to leave the field yet for the fifth time. But it wasn't until about 4:30 when bus riders were ushered onto the buses, the train riders were gathered in the gym, and I left the campus and hurried home that I learned of the magnitude of the disaster. . . .

The problem our family had was that we, in preparing for our move to Thailand in the summer, had already terminated our contract with the TV cable company and thus had no access to the news that the rest of Japan was so intently watching. So I spent the rest of my Friday afternoon slumped in front of the computer, getting updates on the situation through Gmail chat from my Japanese friend, who grimly watched the clips of people and cars being swept away by the tsunami that NHK [Japan Broadcasting Corporation] broadcasted and relayed to me what she learned. Meanwhile, my mom struggled to communicate with my dad, who was stranded at his office and unable to get home. I guess you could attribute it to the fact that, while I had no TV news to watch and couldn't understand the radio, not that we had one, the guilt ate at me when I tried to entertain myself by watching YouTube videos or movies that I ended up lying on my bed from 4:30 in the afternoon until 12:30 in the morning with my eyes glued to a Gmail chat box that blinked orange every few seconds while listening to my mom complain that my dad didn't even want to come home that night for the little effort he'd been putting into finding transportation. I couldn't even sleep, even though my body craved it so much. . . .

Being a Foreigner in Tokyo in a Time of Crisis

After that day, I got nearly nothing done, stuck in a state of limbo, because I was too exhausted from Friday to work, yet too guilty to watch a movie or entertain myself or even sleep properly, instead just reading the news about the tsunami and nuclear power plant issues all day. The news we got from Thailand, CNN, and NHK came from different directions and gave different messages of varying urgency. On the student Facebook earthquake announcement page, people complained that foreigners were overreacting and evacuating the country even though the situation wasn't even dangerous for those in Tokyo. Although I couldn't disagree, I didn't agree either. Why? Because I still had so much contradicting news that I didn't know what to believe. If there was one thing I learned from my own experiences of being in Japan during this time, it was that being a foreigner in Tokyo is not at all easy in times of crisis. After all, the loudspeaker would call out at odd times of the day giving messages about blackouts in Japanese, so we couldn't understand even the messages meant for us specifically, not to mention that people were in such a panic that they went out and polished off the food at the supermarkets so that, for the first time since we came to Japan, we actually saw the supermarket employees wiping the shelves in the middle of the day. With an ob-

> I still had so much contradicting news that I didn't know what to believe.

viously lowered supply of food and the only up to date information about blackouts and trains in Japanese, it's no wonder about half the school population flew overseas. That's about all I have to say, but I don't really have a conclusion yet, because, well, frankly, the blackouts are still expected to go on, and there's still news about radiation and the power plants, so what happens from now is still to be decided.

A Writer Lives Through the Earthquake and Other 2011 Disasters

Lucy Birmingham and David McNeill

In the following viewpoint, a foreign correspondent living in Tokyo describes how she and her coworkers reacted when the automated earthquake warning system sounded on their phones and the shaking of their building grew stronger. She talks about her concern for her children and her efforts to reach them to ensure they were safe. She explains why the Japanese had been warned that it was risky to build nuclear facilities in Japan. She goes on to discuss the situation at the Fukushima nuclear power plant, the mass exodus from Japan it triggered, and her decision to stay behind in Tokyo after her family left. Lucy Birmingham is *Time* magazine's Tokyo-based reporter and an editor and scriptwriter for NHK, Japan's national television and radio broadcaster. David McNeill is the Japan and Korea correspondent for the *Chronicle of Higher Education* and writes regularly for several international publications.

SOURCE. Lucy Birmingham and David McNeill, *Strong in the Rain: Surviving Japan's Earthquake, Tsunami and Fukushima Nuclear Disaster*, published 2012, copyright © Palgrave Macmillan. Reproduced with permission of Palgrave Macmillan.

Just another quake, I mused after sensing a mild trembler roll through the Tokyo NHK [Japan Broadcasting Corporation] newsroom, the national broadcaster where I'd worked since 2000. Seconds before, a cacophony of buzzing cell phones owned by the 60 or so staff in the bustling room had warned of the approaching seism [earthquake]. All Japanese phones are designed with an automated earthquake warning system, and the noisy phone eruption had reminded us once again that we lived on one of the most quake-prone lands on the planet.

But the massive jolt seconds later stopped us in our tracks. This one was different—not the usual back-and-forth roll but an unmistakable hard jump, a sure sign that something more intense was coming our way. I glanced out the window onto the expanse of trees and sky over Yoyogi Park and noticed a dark sweep of clouds quickly covering the patches of blue like a great, ominous warning. Below, two shirtless men were playing basketball, oblivious to the chilly March weather or undulating ground beneath them.

As the shaking intensified, the old headquarters building began to weave with an angry groan. Windows rattled hard and objects fell from shelves. As I followed everyone's lend and jumped under a desk, I discovered a terrified colleague curled in a ball, shaking uncontrollably, eyes brimming with tears. "We'll be all right," I said, trying to calm her, but in truth my confidence was waning fast. This was by far the strongest and longest earthquake I'd ever experienced during my many years in Japan.

> This was by far the strongest and longest earthquake I'd ever experienced during my many years in Japan.

Despair Turns into Relief

My thoughts immediately went to my three teenage children as a growing dread churned into nausea. As if we were caught in a bizarre time warp of terror, the seconds passed like hours while the quake's deep waves whipped like a dragon's tail below us.

When the rattling finally halted and we all emerged from under the desks, I immediately tried to reach my kids by cell phone. But the service was either jammed with calls or suspended. My text messages went unanswered, so I opted for a landline and managed to reach my Japanese in-laws before the lines overloaded with calls.

"Don't worry—we heard from Seiya and he's on his way back home," said my mother-in-law. I breathed a sigh of relief. My 19-year-old was at nearby Shibuya Station just about to step onto a train when the quake hit. Had he done so seconds earlier, it could have meant hours stuck in a packed carriage or worse. I knew my 14-year-old, Sachi, was at a friend's house not far from home. I was confident her friend's parents would take care of her.

That left Nina, my irascible 17-year-old. She was at her high school over an hour away by train, a trip that included two transfers. My heart began to pound as I considered the possibilities. Parents need great faith to live in a vast urban environment. The Greater Tokyo Area is almost the size of Connecticut, and it has a population density twice that of Bangladesh. Fortunately, Tokyo is overall a safe city for children. But in such a violent earthquake, Nina's life was in the hands of fate.

I will never forget Nina's message that arrived at 8:48 P.M.: "I'm fine. I will stay at school tonight." She had attached a photo of her and some friends lying on mats in her classroom. They were among several hundred students, teachers, and parents taking refuge there for the night. In an instant I had gone from growing despair to elated relief. The moment fueled my love and appreciation for my children. It also gave me strength to face the mounting revelations that this was becoming an unprecedented triple disaster.

Learning of the Nuclear Situation

After I got home in the early hours of the next morning, I went to my in-laws' house nearby and found them wide-awake, watching the unfolding news on TV. "This is quite a birthday present," said my father-in-law. Indeed, it was March 12, his eighty-fifth birthday. "I've survived World War II, the [1995] Kobe earthquake, and now one of the worst quakes in Japan's history," he said. "I sure hope this is it for a while."

> For those like him who remembered the atomic bombing of Hiroshima and Nagasaki, there was worse to come.

For those like him who remembered the [World War II] atomic bombing of [the Japanese cities of] Hiroshima and Nagasaki, there was worse to come. The situation at the six-reactor Fukushima Daiichi nuclear power plant in the northeast, 155 miles up the coast from Tokyo, appeared to be worsening. Operator Tokyo Electric Power Company (TEPCO) announced at 6:45 A.M. that radioactive substances may have leaked from the plant.

With limited natural resources and a reluctance to depend on foreign oil, the country's energy policy had been steered toward nuclear since the 1960s, despite being the only country in the world to experience atomic bombings. Deep government backing and close ties with the industry had set its policy in stone at that time: 30 percent nuclear with plans to increase to 50 percent by 2030. There were 55 reactors in various stages of operation and plans to build more. Serious accidents at several plants had occurred amid claims of cover-ups and falsified safety reports.

Geologists had warned of the enormous risks of building in such a seismically unstable country. But it was promoted as a safe, clean energy source, and resistance among the general population was minimal. In areas where nuclear power plants were proposed, local governments squelched the naysayers with money. The Fukushima plant, commissioned in 1971, brought jobs to the Tohoku area, known for its stagnant growth, depopulation, and historic poverty. Not a single watt of the electricity generated there was used in Fukushima. It all served Tokyo. Now the people of that prefecture were about to pay a terrible price for the deal they had made.

The Exodus

By Sunday morning, two days after the quake and tsunami, the news began to percolate among the foreign community that radiation carried from Fukushima in the wind and water might reach Tokyo. Rumors were circulating that embassies had recommended their citizens to get out of Tokyo, and even Japan altogether.

The exodus alarm went off on Sunday evening when the French embassy e-mailed its citizens a recommendation that they leave the Tokyo area. Other European countries quickly followed its lead. Later that week, the international schools began closing, kicking the fear factor into full gear. The US 7th Fleet moved its ships, aircraft, and personnel into open sea, away from Tokyo, because its equipment detected high radiation.

> The exodus ruffled feathers in a country that can still feel closed, even xenophobic, and where distrust of foreign intentions is seldom far from the surface.

The exodus ruffled feathers in a country that can still feel closed, even xenophobic, and where distrust of foreign intentions is seldom far from the surface. There were grumbles from within many companies, domestic and international, that the Japanese staff was feeling abandoned. The term *flyjin*, a word based on the mildly derogatory term *gaijin* for foreigners, began to appear. But the mass exodus clogging roadways, airports, and train stations wasn't just a foreigner phenomenon. It involved anyone who could afford to leave, which included plenty of Japanese.

Some in the banking community flew out on privately chartered jets. For most everyone else, it was long waits at immigration, in ticket lines, and at gasoline stands. The southwest region of Kansai, mainly Kyoto, Osaka, and Kobe, became the refuge of choice. Some international companies shuttered Tokyo offices to set up temporarily in Osaka, booking hotel suites and conference rooms. Hotels that had emptied just after the March 11 quake refilled with the fleeing people.

Saying Good-bye

On Thursday, my children left with their father, his parents, and the dog for the Kansai region. It seemed the safest and most responsible decision. As a journalist, I felt it was my responsibility to stay in Tokyo. But saying good-bye was one of the toughest moments I've ever had. As I choked back tears, my mind raced with questions. Would this be the last time I'd see them? Was Tokyo really at risk of becoming a radioactive wasteland, as some media had reported? Was I signing away my future to cancer? Was I being a responsible parent?

Just at that moment, Nina surprised me with a heartfelt hug. Tears welled in her eyes as she then handed me a box of protective face masks. "Mom, you'll be okay. But just make sure you wear a mask," she said firmly. I winced at the thought and then promised her I'd at least try one on. "We'll get through this," she added with a smile. It was then that I realized that her generation would be the bearers of this tragedy. Would they be able to change their world?

A Japanese Evacuee Shares Her Concerns

Izumi Nakano

In the following viewpoint, a head nurse in a facility close to the Fukushima Daiichi Nuclear Power Plant describes the challenges she has faced since March 11, 2011. Ordered to evacuate the area in which she lived because of the nuclear meltdown, she and her husband moved from one evacuation center to another. She explains how troubled she was about her patients and about the situation regarding nursing care for evacuees. She relates how her religion helped her find the strength not to give up and deepen her compassion for her patients. She shares what she did to make her patients begin to open up and confide in her and explains why, in spite of the hardships she has had to endure, she feels fulfilled. Izumi Nakano is a nursing care manager from Iwaki City, Fukushima Prefecture Japan.

SOURCE. Izumi Nakano, "Learning to Listen from the Heart," *Seikyo Shimbun*, February 11. 2012, Soka Gakkai International. Copyright © 2012 by the Seikyo Shimbun. All rights reserved. Reproduced by permission.

I am a nursing care manager and one of my responsibilities is to put together care plans tailored specifically to the individual needs of people who require nursing care. This involves both consulting the patients and liaising with nursing establishments to ensure patients receive the care they need.

My home is in the town of Futaba, 4 kilometers from Fukushima Daiichi Nuclear Power Plant. The area that I worked in also lies within a 20 kilometer radius of the nuclear plant. The March 11, 2011, earthquake and subsequent tsunami caused three of the reactors at the power plant to go into meltdown. As a result, all residents were ordered to evacuate the area and my husband and I were forced to move from one evacuation center to the next.

Following the evacuation, I was beside myself with worry as I didn't know what had happened to my patients. There was no way to contact them, so all I could do was to pray earnestly for their safety.

> Following the evacuation, I was beside myself with worry as I didn't know what had happened to my patients.

Trying to Help in Difficult Times

As time passed, I began to hear about the dreadful conditions that patients were being subjected to. For example, one bed-ridden lady, despite not being fit enough to withstand being moved, was denied admission to the first evacuation center she was taken to as it was already full. As she had to be evacuated from the 20 kilometer zone, she was taken by bus to the next shelter. However, the journey took many hours, and, sadly, she was found dead on arrival, having passed away in the passenger seat. Another patient who sought refuge outside Fukushima prefecture was taken to a long-term care facility but when the staff there found out that he had come from Fukushima, they feared he had been contaminated by radiation and turned him away.

It was finally at the end of April that I was able to settle down in Iwaki City. Since then, I have been engaged in helping locate those who had previously lived in nursing homes and find temporary residences for them. I worked with the municipalities and nursing care facilities to ensure the smooth transfer of residents. Soon after, I was assigned to look after evacuees in Iwaki City who require nursing care.

Following the unrest surrounding the nuclear accident, the situation regarding evacuees in need of nursing care was extremely difficult. The stress of starting a new life in an unfamiliar place, as well as having to live in cramped, temporary housing, weighed heavily on care givers and care receivers alike, so much so that it caused discord among family members. Countless patients expressed sentiments such as: "Ever since being brought to this shelter, I've lost all motivation" or, "I don't know anybody here. I am so lonely." Desperately yearning to return to their homes, yet not being able to do so, these patients gradually lost hope and with it, their will to live. In some cases, patients even lost their physical strength to the extent that they could no longer walk.

> Desperately yearning to return to their homes, yet not being able to do so, these patients gradually lost hope and with it, their will to live.

What I found most agonizing was how, although I wished to listen to their struggles, the patients would not easily open up and confide in me. Many of them suffered in silence because they felt that no one could understand their predicament.

Sometimes, on the way home from work, I wished I could return to my hometown of Futaba and I would break down and cry. However, thanks to the support and encouragement of fellow Soka Gakkai [international Buddhist movement] members, I was able to get through these difficult times.

A Change in Attitude

I spurred myself on by telling myself that now was the time to utilize my Buddhist practice and, as I began chanting Nam-myoho-renge-kyo earnestly, a shift began to take place in my attitude toward patients. I resolved to wholeheartedly encourage each person and to reassure them that they were not alone in their struggle. I also made efforts to visit patients more frequently to offer support. I decided to chant until I reached a positive breakthrough in my relationship with each and every one of them.

I began to talk less and listen more. At other times, I exchanged friendly banter with patients and tried to make them laugh. Gradually, they began to open up and to confide in me.

One day, one of my patients, an elderly woman, sobbed as I held her in my arms. She thought she was of no use to others and a burden upon her family. She said she wished she had died on the day of the earthquake. I comforted her and told her that what she was saying was not true and that just being alive is, in itself, wondrous— that human life is the most precious thing we have. We both wept together and at that moment I felt as though I could see a faint light at the end of a dark tunnel. When I am able to encourage those that have gone through similar experiences and hardships as I have, I feel optimistic. I feel as though my experience of living in evacuation shelters has not been in vain. Needless to say, my day-to-day life remains challenging. However, I feel deep fulfillment when I think about how overcoming my own struggles can give hope to others.

I re-encountered the old lady who had wept in my arms following our first meeting. She was in high spirits

> When I am able to encourage those that have gone through similar experiences and hardships as I have, I feel optimistic.

and had been able to reconnect with her family and have heartfelt conversation with them. She asked me if I would be willing to listen to her if she ever needed my help again. I replied, with a big smile, that next time I would like to seek her advice!

After the Disaster: A Return to a Devastated Japan

David Baresch

In the following viewpoint, a British educator who left Japan after the 2011 earthquake recounts his experiences upon his return a few months later. While on a train heading toward the area hit by the tsunami, he recalls his memories of muddied Japanese rice fields. He describes the landscape—the fractures that scar the streets and the mounds of household wreckage from tsunami-hit homes—as he makes his way through a quiet town toward a seawall. He goes on to recount the horrible scenes of disaster and loss he views from his taxi window as he travels into the tsunami-hit area. He shares his feelings about the changes wrought by the earthquake and tsunami and, after running into a group of Japanese teens, ponders what effect the tragedy might have on their lives. David Baresch is an English-language teacher in Saitama, Japan.

SOURCE. David Baresch, "After the Disaster: A Return to a Devastated Japan," *Contemporary Review,* vol. 293, no. 1702, September 2011, pp. 317–320. Copyright © 2011 by Contemporary Review. All rights reserved. Reproduced by permission.

The train headed towards the tsunami-hit area. Here, acres of rice fields met my eyes. My thoughts returned to newsreels shown in the days after the great earthquake. I remembered an aerial view of a fleeing car. The car sped along a road that cut through farmland, similar to that which now passed by. A mass of sea-water rushed in from the left. It had already spread across the road behind the vehicle. The driver accelerated forward, intent on making a rapid escape, but, from our view from above, we could see that the incoming wave was pincer shaped. The driver was unaware that he, or she, was racing towards the other arm of the tsunami.

Without warning, a great wall of water stormed across the road, about one hundred metres ahead of the car. The driver braked hard. The vehicle angled sharply to the left and stopped.

Perhaps the driver was now fully aware of his predicament. An encompassing wave was flooding in from the front, the back, and the left. On the right lay muddied rice fields. Trapped.

The car remained motionless. What was going through the driver's mind at that moment? Seemingly, he had run out of ideas. The car remained motionless.

In the same shot, someone else was seen racing through the fields, trying to outrun the tsunami. The footage ended. Such are my memories of rice fields.

The train chugged on and passed through small towns. Most roofs had been damaged and were patched up with blue tarpaulin. Aftershocks are expected to continue for another couple of years yet. So, plastic sheets are used as makeshift roofs for the time being.

Matsushima was the next and final station. On this stretch of track, the train rattled through a string of tunnels. With thoughts of the earthquake and tsunami in mind, claustrophobia hit. The tunnels seemed unnervingly long. I sensed relief whenever we exited into the bright sunlight and, greater relief still, when I stepped off the train and onto the platform at Matsushima Station.

It was a warm, sunny, spring day, the sky clear blue, typical of Japan. The small station seemed to have been untouched by the disaster. It was inconceivable that I was just a few kilometres from one of the world's worst ever tragedies.

> " It was inconceivable that I was just a few kilometres from one of the world's worst ever tragedies. "

I made my way through the sleepy town. Here and there, snaking fractures scarred the streets. On each side of the breaks the land had either been lifted or had sunk. Jagged steps of about 25cm in height had formed and were surrounded by safety-cones. In other places, heaps of fallen masonry had been shovelled up against walls. Suddenly, the smell of dust, mixed with damp burnt wood, filled the air. Here, mounds of household wreckage met my eyes.

A sport's field, consisting of two football pitches and a baseball diamond, was being used as a dumping ground to separate the wreckage from the tsunami-hit homes. There were mounds of wood, mounds of bedding and sofas, mounds of twisted metals, mounds [of] colourful plastics, and all were clumped together and coated in dust.

The biggest mound was that of, yet to be sorted, debris, which looked like a pile of giant jigsaw pieces. Familiar objects poked out at odd, undignified, angles. Mickey Mouse, his lower body ensnared, grinned and waved his one free arm. CDs glinted and caught the eye. 'Hello Kitty', dressed in her most shocking pink, craned forward as if gasping for air. Brightly coloured towels and curtains entwined computers, chairs, and tables. Partially trapped futons spewed forward and flopped down as if in exhaustion. And all were bound and knotted together under the weight of a great disaster.

The jumbled lives of so many could be seen dumped onto that playing field in Matsushima; and what of the occupants?

Treading carefully over cracks, gaps, and uplifted masonry, I reached the seawall. Here, I rested and took in the scene. A string of small leafy islands dotted the horizon. I sat for a while and listened to the whispers of the gentle waves.

'Taxi! Can you take me to the tsunami-hit area?' I showed the driver my ID. He smiled broadly, nodded, and switched the metre on, a typical response of Japanese staff facing customer.

We drove past scenic costal views. Here was, undoubtedly, a major Japanese beauty spot. After some time, we reached a long downhill stretch of road. We were nearing lower lying land, and the terrain susceptible to tsunamis.

> From out of nowhere, a blackened, muddied, myriad of destruction emerged.

The taxi sped on. Trees blurred by. The calm sea lay behind. And within that blur of green, I caught a glimpse of a car, upended, and buried in the roof of a house. We had reached the disaster zone.

From out of nowhere, a blackened, muddied, myriad of destruction emerged. A length of railway line had been uplifted by the tsunami and now stood on end, resembling a fence. Masked soldiers rummaged through rubble. Mechanical diggers sharply twisted and jerked. The roads were partially flooded. The smell of dust and damp burnt wood filled the air. A slaughtered, mangled, town lay before me.

The taxi's tyres swished as we drove on over a tarmac of sludge. The driver carefully made his way through pockets of flood water, up to about 30 cm deep in places. Military vehicles shunted to and fro. We pulled over and stopped several times to give way. As we waited, I looked around at the horror.

Houses lining the road had been either ripped apart, flattened, or had gone, carried away on the high seas. Beached boats had pummelled their way through walls. They protruded, like unexploded missiles, half in and half out of battered bedrooms, kitchens and lounges. Crumpled cars lay crippled. Felled telegraph poles balanced on top of mounds of rubble. Gaping holes exposed shattered living rooms. Curtains flapped wildly out of broken windows and doorways as if in a plea for help. And what of the occupants?

We passed by what once had been a river, but now a stream of black sludge. The concrete banks, high and steep, were coated in mire. On the riverbed, rusting coaches, cars, and lorries lay toppled, angled this way and that, as though in exhaustion, having given up an immense struggle, they had turned over, lain down, and died.

How had they arrived at their final resting place? What had been the drivers' and passengers' destinations? Who had been waiting for them? Where had they come from? Who had smiled, and waved good-bye, and said, 'See you later'?

'What's the name of this place?' I asked the taxi driver.

'Ton-na', he cheerfully replied. I wondered what thoughts were hidden behind his broad, friendly smile.

The smell of dust, and damp burnt wood, filled the taxi, and stayed with us as we headed back towards the station. It was a smell that lingered with me for several days. It is a smell that returns whenever I think about Ton-na.

I asked the driver to stop by the sea. I got out and took a long stroll. The tide was in. Moored fishing boats gently rocked and knocked against each other. The seawater was about three metres below the top of the seawall. I looked around at the houses very nearby. I wondered.

Small, uninhabited, islands lay about a kilometre from the shore. They looked serene, covered in deep green foliage, a haven for wildlife. But, my mind constantly wandered back to the tragedy of that cold mid-March afternoon. I remembered newsreels showing entire towns being lifted up by the sea and dashed asunder. My thoughts were a blur of beauty, death, peace and destruction.

> "My thoughts were a blur of beauty, death, peace and destruction."

I walked back towards the station. My head bowed in thought. I was awoken by a bright, 'Hello'. A young Japanese boy, about ten years old, with his friends, jumped at the opportunity to greet a native English speaker. Cheerily, I replied likewise. His face lit up. His friends giggled and muttered as they continued on their way. Perhaps that had made their day.

About fifty teenage schoolgirls waited for the train. They chatted, groomed their hair, and checked their appearances in small mirrors. I felt sure that they must have known people who had either been killed in the disaster, or who were still missing. I wondered what effect such a massive tragedy was having, or would have, on their lives. There was always the possibility of the same occurrence again, here, at any time.

Everyone I came across seemed to be coping fine. But the Japanese are masters at hiding their woes. I could do no more than wonder.

A Journalist Visits the Fukushima Nuclear Plant

Martin Fackler

In the following viewpoint, a reporter recounts his visit to the Fukushima nuclear plant about eight months after the March 2011 disaster. He describes what he saw on the drive that he and a select group of other reporters took to the plant and details the steady rise of the readings on his radiation detector the closer they got to their destination. He then relates what he witnessed inside the plant, from the four-story water tanks full of contaminated seawater and the water decontamination facility to the condition of the damaged reactor buildings, where his radiation reader revealed the highest reading of his visit. He goes on to describe the time-consuming process he and the others underwent entering the disaster center and the scene in the center's Response Room. Martin Fackler is the Tokyo bureau chief for the *New York Times*.

SOURCE. Martin Fackler, "Eyewitness Report—Inside the Wreckage of Japan's Fukushima Nuclear Reactor," *The Telegraph,* November 12, 2011. Copyright © 2011 Telegraph Media Group Limited 2011.

I was one of around three dozen journalists put onto two buses. We were given protective suits, double gloves, a double layer of clear plastic booties over shoes, hair cover, respirator mask and a radiation detector.

And then we began our drive to the plant.

First, we passed through the police check point. Through the bus window, I saw the empty towns of Naraha, Tomioka and Okuma pass by. There were abandoned homes. A plant store with its greenery still on display outside, but withered and dead.

I could see that many homes had been visited and fixed already by residents, with the surrounding areas swept clean and debris from the earthquake placed into neat piles.

Other houses, however, were clearly left exactly as they were when residents fled on March 11. Inside one office, I saw papers scattered in piles on the floor, apparently untouched since the earthquake.

We continued past a pachinko [Japanese gambling device like a pinball machine] parlour, its façade collapsed, and a car dealership with its windows shattered and insulation exposed.

Then came a gas station which had been cleaned up of debris—but then taken over by a population of crows.

All the time, I watched the radiation readings on my detector rise steadily as we approached the [Fukushima Daiichi nuclear] plant: it read 0.7 microsieverts per hour in Naraha, located just near the edge of the 12 mile restricted zone from the plant.

Rising Radiation Levels

As we reached Tomioka, it rose to 0.9, and then soon it was 1.5. In Tomioka, we passed a former welcome centre for nuclear plants operated by Tokyo Electric Power Station (TEPCO), operators of Fukushima Daiichi.

It consisted of a small collection of Bavarian-style gingerbread buildings.

There was even a poster of Naoto Kan, the prime minister at the time of March 11, who is now no longer in power.

By now, the warning buzzer on my radiation detector was going off constantly: I watched the radiation levels rise quickly, from 2.7 microsieverts to 3.7 to 4.1.

When we arrived in a place called Okuma, the reading was 6.7 microsieverts and the bus came to a halt. We were instructed to put on respirator masks at this stage—which meant that every inch of my skin was now covered and protected.

Then we turned onto the main road which leads to the plant. We were within 3 kilometres of the plant at this stage but even here, many houses appeared to be neat, with front doors closed, window curtains drawn.

Finally, we reached the security checkpoint at the entrance of the plant: the radiation detector buzzed at 20 microsieverts.

Inside the Nuclear Plant

Then we were inside the plant: the first journalists in Japan permitted to visit since the March 11 disaster.

The first thing visible were half a dozen large cranes dominating the skyline. Next, we passed a field filled with blue train-car like tanks for holding contaminated water.

There were also dozens of large, four storey silver tanks, also containing contaminated sea water.

According to TEPCO, there are 90,000 tons of water stored here, after [being] cleaned, with plans to build more storage.

Workers were visible at this point building new water tanks—as the day I visited was a Saturday, they were among 1,600 workers at the plant, around half of the 3,200 present daily during the week.

> According to TEPCO [Tokyo Electric Power Company], there are 90,000 tons of water stored here, after [being] cleaned, with plans to build more storage.

Journalists are given a tour of the Fukushima Daiichi power plant in full radioactive protective gear in November 2011. (© David Guttenfelder/AFP/Getty Images.)

The next thing to catch my eye was a cluster of white tents surrounded by black sand bags, which apparently help protect workers inside from radiation.

This was the water decontamination facility, its entrance marked with US, French and Japanese flags.

As we drove through the grounds, I saw that it was filled with pine forest, giving it an almost bucolic feel.

Viewing the Reactor Buildings

Finally, we got our first proper look at the damaged reactor buildings. No 1 was covered by a new superstructure, No 2 was intact. No 3 was in worst shape: it was a skeletal frame, largely collapsed into a pile of rubble.

I spotted three cranes clearing up rubble at No 3, in preparation for also capping off that building with a superstructure.

No 4 was also severely damaged. The building was intact, but it had clearly buckled, with concrete slabs blown out. The entire south side of the building was blown out, exposing the green crane for spent fuel rod pool.

At this point, around 1,640 feet from the reactors, I stopped to check my radiation reader: 50 microsieverts per hour.

> Most of the grounds of the plant are located 98 feet above sea level, but the reactors are located on a lower shelf-like area only 32 feet above sea level.

Despite the radiation levels, there were signs of life still in the plant grounds: I spotted crows and dragonflies through the bus windows.

Most of the grounds of the plant are located 98 feet above sea level, but the reactors are located on a lower shelf-like area only 32 feet above sea level.

Arriving at the base of the reactor buildings, we could clearly see the damage was still not cleared up from the tsunami and the hydrogen explosions.

My eyes took in crumpled trucks, twisted metal girders and frames of buildings, a huge storage tank dented and bent.

Pipes on the side of the building had been twisted and pulled off, and remained hanging.

The damage reached as high as the second storey, attesting to the height of the tsunami.

Our buses drove between the reactors and the sea. I noticed a 13 feet sea wall built with rocks in black nets, which TEPCO said was a makeshift defence against future tsunami.

A glance at my radiation reader revealed the levels were 300 microsieverts per hour—the highest reading of my visit.

The base of the reactor buildings was filled with debris, the sort familiar to anyone who has seen the damage caused by the tsunami in other areas: lots of twisted metal, including three white cars with TEPCO markings crushed together.

There were twisted trucks fallen into empty pools and an office building left gutted by the tsunami.

Next, we headed back up by bus towards a place called the "Seismic Safety Building"—the plant disaster's headquarters.

As we drove there, we saw further evidence of the scale of the earthquake's damage: big cracks in the earth, buckled metal shutters on buildings, toppled sheds.

Entering the Disaster Centre

Then, we entered the disaster centre. Entering was a time-consuming process, due to radioactivity precautions.

In the first room, lined with pink plastic sheets, we took off our booties.

Then, in the next room, teams of workers cut off our protective suits with scissors, removed our gloves and masks.

Inside, I could hear the roar of air filters. A quick radiation reading check revealed 1.5 microsieverts per hour. I saw long strings of paper cranes, posters and even hand towels with messages of support for plant workers from around Japan and a few from the United States.

Next, we went into the Response Room, the plant's crisis centre. This was a large room, filled with men alone as no women are permitted to work at the plant due to health reasons.

One wall was filled with screens, most showing live images from around the plant. A group of 25 men were sitting around an oval of tables at the front of the room, with another dozen tables filling the rest of the space, filled with men tapping at laptops.

At the head of the room was a white board listing temperatures and hydrogen readings of the six reactors. And on another wall, there was a small plain wood Shinto [Japanese religion] shrine.

Here, Goshi Hosono, the minister in charge of the nuclear crisis clean up, dressed in his blue workmen clothes, came to address workers.

"Every time I come back, I feel conditions have improved," he said. "This is due to your hard work."

Tracking Tsunami Flotsam

Marcus Erikson

In the following viewpoint, an expert in plastic marine pollution describes the sea voyage in which he and a team of eleven others took part in 2012. The objective was to track the March 11, 2011, tsunami debris, study the factors affecting its path, and assess its ecological effects. The author shares information on the debris and on the team's findings, including what determines where and when debris arrives and what makes a piece react differently to wind and current. He details what they captured by trawling and what kinds of debris they observed and recorded, including three objects from the tsunami—a tire from a small truck, a piece of a traditional tatami mat, and part of a crushed fishing boat. Marcus Erikson is the executive director and cofounder of the 5 Gyres Institute, an organization dedicated to ending plastics pollution in the world's oceans.

SOURCE. Marcus Erikson, "Tracking Tsunami Flotsam," *Natural Museum Magazine,* July–August 2012. Copyright © 2012 by American Museum of Natural History. All rights reserved. Reproduced by permission.

On June 10, 2012, fifteen months after the tsunami of March 11 that ravaged the east coast of northern Japan, we drop our dock lines and depart Yokohama Bay. Our expedition is leaving ten days later than planned, thanks to Mawar, the first typhoon of the season. With the tropical depression that will become Typhoon Guchol forming off the Philippines, we have chosen to squeeze between the two storms and race 1,000 miles offshore to clear the Kuroshio Current. Like the Gulf Stream of the North Atlantic, the Kuroshio is a warm-water highway that big storms track, northward along Japan's eastern shore. We are a team of a dozen sailors, scientists, photographers, journalists, and environmentalists representing eight different countries. Standing on the bow of Sea Dragon, the seventy-two-foot racing sailboat we chartered to Hawaii, we are smiling for now. Our experienced skipper, Rodrigo Olson from Ensenada, Mexico, has previously sailed the equivalent distance of ten circumnavigations around the equator. I trust him when he says, "Let's go. It could get rough, so we need to sail east, fast."

> The tsunami washed entire communities, an estimated 5 million tons of material, into the ocean at one time, on one day.

The tsunami washed entire communities, an estimated 5 million tons of material, into the ocean at one time, on one day. Some 16,000 thousand lives were confirmed lost, with at least 3,000 more still unaccounted for. During our weather delay in Japan, we traveled to Fukushima to volunteer with a relief agency helping some citizens briefly enter their homes in the no-go zone around the damaged nuclear reactors. Low levels of radioactivity allowed people to return, but we still brought our own Geiger counter. More than 150 miles of the coastline is stripped bare. Concrete slabs lie where homes once stood, much of the debris gathered into giant piles to be separated manually into recoverable materials. But much more was washed into the Pacific, and what didn't sink immediately was taken by the Kuroshio Current into the North Pacific Subtropical Gyre, an ocean-wide vortex of clockwise currents that sequester floating trash.

> As horrible as that disaster was, it has also provided scientists with an opportunity to learn something new, a unique and unrepeatable experiment in oceanography.

As horrible as that disaster was, it has also provided scientists with an opportunity to learn something new, a unique and unrepeatable experiment in oceanography. Of all the construction material, metals, roofing tiles, insulation, cars, tires, trees, glass bulbs, appliances, furniture, textiles, and diverse plastic materials, what, we want to know, is still at sea today, and where is it going? Natural organics, such as trees and wooden construction materials, are likely gone, bored by worms or waterlogged and sunk. Metals, glass, and fiberglass, unless still trapping air, have also sunk, leaving mostly polyethylene and polypropylene plastics adrift. With tremendous caution and compassion, we are going to find out.

Two California-based organizations, the 5 Gyres Institute in Santa Monica and the Algalita Marine Research Institute in Long Beach, organized the expedition route based on oceanographic models predicting landfall of tsunami debris.

To date hundreds of tsunami artifacts have reached the shore from northern California to Kodiak, Alaska, including oyster-farm floats, soccer balls, a fishing dock, one Harley-Davidson in the back of an insulated container, and a 120-foot rusted fishing boat (which was scuttled soon after its discovery near British Columbia). Based on the videos of debris being swept off Japan the year before, the public imagines a haunting mirror image, with waves of debris crashing onshore. But when and where debris arrives depends on a variety of factors, especially variations in the direction and velocity of wind and current.

That's not all. "What we're finding is that debris reacts differently to wind and current depending on how it is positioned in the water," explained Nikolai Maximenko of the International Pacific Research Center of the University of Hawaii, an oceanographer tracking tsunami debris. In other words, the movement of a floating object depends on how much of it is exposed to the wind, known as its windage, and how much is beneath the surface. "What you may find on your expedition is the low-windage, subsurface debris field," he said. We want to ground-truth this model, as well as to understand the life cycle of diverse materials thrust into the ocean: what marine life colonizes this debris, and what the long-term ecological impacts are.

We have one more assignment. Weeks before our departure date we received a call from the Woods Hole Oceanographic Institute in Massachusetts. "Looks like you're following the same route we sailed last year to study radioactive fallout from the Fukushima reactor," senior scientist Ken Buesseler informed us. "Could you revisit the same sites?" Ten flat-packing twenty-liter bottles soon arrived. The work is simple: fill them with seawater from stations every 5 degrees of longitude. Buesseler will analyze these months later in his lab using sensitive detection equipment to screen for low-level radiation. In 2011 Buesseler and other scientists detected cesium-134 (^{134}Cs), a radioactive isotope of the element, along their Tokyo-to-Hawaii transect, with a spike at 170 degrees East longitude, but still far below levels threatening to humans. They want to know if it's moved—and if it's detectable at all. This isotope has a half-life of two years, so in ten years, or five half-lives, 97 percent of it decays. Any ^{134}Cs in the Pacific Ocean today is from Fukushima, since any source of it from nuclear testing half a century ago is long gone.

We're sailing 3,800 nautical miles to get to the debris field, which at the time of our voyage is centered at 35 degrees North and the international date line. It's as far from land as you can get on the planet without leaving the surface. We do no research for the first five days, focused on getting miles under our belt. With 100-knot sustained winds circulating in a storm that moves four times as fast as we do, there is no room for error. The sea always has the last word.

The first few days of the expedition are wrought with nausea, caffeine-deprivation headaches (because you can't stomach even the smell of coffee), and bruises from navigating narrow passageways inside what sometimes feels like a washing machine. With a break in the weather, we deploy our high-speed trawl, a net we designed to skim the sea surface at speeds up to eight knots. With an opening five and a half inches wide by eighteen inches tall and a 500-micron-mesh net, it captures zooplankton, fish, and plastic. Today's catch unveils a few unusual suspects. Among the flying fish, squid, salps, and jellies, we find a paper nautilus, Argonauta argo (a species of octopus); a pelagic nudibranch, or sea slug, Glaucus atlanticus (also known as the sea swallow); Pacific viperfish (Chauliodus macouni); and several lanternfishes. These last fish (family Myctophidae), we've discovered in previous research, ingest microplastic particles, a multi-colored panorama of which, undistinguishable as to product or country of origin, makes up the bulk in terms of weight of what the trawl collects.

With a careful eye on the skies, we plot a course eastward between 30 and 32 degrees North for 2,000 miles through the southern half of the tsunami debris field. The two cyclones have withered, but then merged to create a persistent low-pressure system above 35 degrees North, requiring us to stay to its south. Crew keep busy trawling the seas for plastic, and first mate Jesse Horton becomes adept at scooping up debris from the bow, netting

Photo on previous page: A mass of floating debris and trash accumulates against the bay of Rukuzentakata on the northeast coast of Japan on March 14, 2011. (© The Asahi Shimbun/Getty Images.)

a toothbrush and a comb within one hour, and occasionally a fragment with identifiable Japanese characters. We've begun timed observations. With a clipboard and a stopwatch, two people stare at the sea surface out to sixty feet off the beam on both sides, recording everything they see. In forty-one nonconsecutive hours spread over three weeks, we catalog 690 pieces, averaging one piece every 3.6 minutes. We also record 130 random observations of trash, all identified as to object and material when possible.

> "Only 2 percent of the [recovered] items are non-plastic, including glass, metal, and natural organics."

Only 2 percent of the items are non-plastic, including glass, metal, and natural organics. Roughly 60 percent are unidentified fragments of hard plastic or foamed polystyrene. The rest are unmistakable items: buckets, crates, flip-flops, a coffee cup, fishing floats and rope, plastic bags and bottles, bottle caps, a toy red pail in the shape of a castle, a syringe, a clothes hanger, a surfboard fin, a felt-tip marker, a boot eerily laced to the top, and a few glass jars, bottles, bulbs, and fluorescent tubes. It's extremely difficult to know when or from where debris has originated, but three objects stand out as from the tsunami.

"A big tire just went by!" photographer Mandy Barker yells. We go back for it. It is not easy to turn the boat around when full sails are up. "Roll the jib and center the main," skipper Olson yells. Barker keeps her eyes on the tire, now more than a tenth of a mile behind us. "Ten degrees to port, fifty meters off the bow," crew yell to guide the boat to the tire. Using a scoop net, it's a struggle to haul the algae-covered tire aboard, still inflated on the rim. Thirty small crabs drop to the deck. A bristle worm is wedged between the rim and the tire, and a dozen gooseneck barnacles sticking outward along the treads flail their cirri, or legs, grasping at the air. It's a tire from a small truck, unlike a tire seen on U.S. vehicles, with "Made in Japan" embossed on one side. The rim is well preserved where it is painted, but any exposed iron is nearly rusted through. If left for another year in the sea, the tire would likely fill with water and sink.

Soon after, Paul Sharp, founder of Australia's Two Hands Project, nets a piece of thatch the size of a large pizza box. Two layers of straw thatch, factory stitched with a thin sheet of blue foamed polystyrene insulation in the middle, is unmistakably a piece of traditional tatami mat from the floor of a Japanese home. Straw, like any other natural organic or wooden construction material, does not last long at sea. Wood-boring worms, known to plague ships for centuries, or seawater seeping into the air-trapping spaces between plant tissues, will decrease the buoyancy of plant material and eventually sink it. The timing of decay, location in the debris field, and lack of slow-growing colonial bryozoans give me confidence that the tire and matting are from the tsunami.

"I think it's a whale!" one crewmember says, followed seconds later with, "No, it's a capsized boat." In the late afternoon, 1,587 nautical miles east of Tokyo, we discover the forward half of a crushed fishing boat drifting in the water. Any excitement at finding it is muted by the real possibility that this boat belonged to someone who suffered—and perhaps perished—in the tsunami. I dive in with the skipper to investigate and film fish aggregating below. We count at least eight species, including amberjack, mahi mahi, and a pair of wahoo. They disperse as I approach. I grab the rail of the boat for a closer look, and see that the hull and deck are remarkably barren of colonizing marine life. Expecting a bouquet of gooseneck barnacles, crabs, nudibranchs, and polychaete worms, I find only eight adult barnacles on the entire exposed surface, which sits two-thirds below the sea surface. In one small, protected crack I see the diversity I am looking for, hidden from grazing triggerfish. We haul the boat aboard and immediately send photographs to NHK Broadcasting in Japan. The three characters in the boat's name are literally translated as "bright," "door," and "vessel." By the end of our trip, the photographs are broadcast on Japanese television in search of the owner (still unidentified to date).

On day sixteen of our expedition, rounding the northwest end of the Papahānaumokuākea Marine National Monument, we exit the tsunami debris field. The national monument is a 139,797-square-mile conservation area that encompasses most of the string of minor Hawaiian Islands. After sailing the remaining 1,200 nautical miles to Honolulu, Hawaii, I meet Nikolai Maximenko in a coffee shop. His latest animations track tsunami debris with variations in windage. I show him the debris we found, all of which fits the low-windage profile. We realize that much of the debris hasn't made it across the ocean yet. But that doesn't mean we'll see an avalanche of trash anytime soon. Comparing the high-windage debris model with that of low windage, we see they do not go in the same direction. "By early summer 2012 we've witnessed most of the high-windage debris make its way across, pushed by wind to the shores of Alaska, British Columbia, Washington, and Oregon," Maximenko explains.

> We realize that much of the debris hasn't made it across the ocean yet.

Low-windage debris, influenced largely by current, behaves differently, moving southward into the California Current and the Great Pacific Garbage Patch. What we'll likely see in the years ahead is a trickle of debris reaching North American coastlines, and then an increase in degraded-plastic pollution on the eastern shores of Hawaii, like famed Kamilo and Kahuku beaches, where weekly beach cleanups can barely keep up with the never-ending plastic waves. Over time the tsunami debris will become indistinguishable from the background of trash in the North Pacific Subtropical Gyre, noticeable only as an increase in microplastics in future researchers' trawls. The impacts on wildlife owing to ingestion and entanglement are the same, whatever the source.

The immediate response to the 2011 tsunami has been to care for the victims and pick up the pieces. But that natural disaster will continue to leave its mark on distant shores—and it's mostly plastic.

GLOSSARY

5 Gyres Institute	A marine conservation nonprofit organization concerned with marine plastic pollution worldwide.
dojo	A school or practice hall where martial arts are taught.
flyjin	Scornful Japanese term for people who fled Japan because of the Fukushima nuclear disaster.
GDP (gross domestic product)	The total value of goods produced and services provided in a country during one year.
isolation condenser	At the Fukushima nuclear plant, a system that cools a reactor when ordinary pumps—powered by such alternating-current sources as outside power supplies and emergency generators—cannot operate.
jishuku	Japanese term meaning self-restraint.
kanji	One of the four writing systems used in modern Japanese.
Kantei	Office of the Japanese prime minister and his cabinet.
Kyoto	City in the central part of the island of Honshu, Japan, that until the mid-nineteenth century was the imperial capital of Japan.
millisievert (mSv)	Measure of radiation dose and exposure.
Nam-myoho-renge-kyo	The Lotus Sutra, which, when chanted regularly, is believed by Buddhists to be a means of improving health, happiness, wisdom, and compassion.
NGO (nongovernmental organization)	Any nonprofit voluntary citizens' group organized on a local, national, or international level.

NHK (Japan Broadcasting Corporation)	Japan's public broadcasting organization.
NOAA (National Oceanic and Atmospheric Administration)	US federal agency focused on the condition of the oceans and the atmosphere.
NRC (Nuclear Regulatory Commission)	US federal agency that licenses and regulates the nation's civilian use of radioactive materials.
nuclear reactor	Device that converts energy stored in atoms into heat or electricity.
Operation Tomodachi	Effort launched by the US armed forces to provide relief to disaster victims of the March 2011 Japan earthquake and tsunami.
Pacific Gyre	One of five major gyres—circular ocean currents formed by the earth's wind patterns and the forces created by the rotation of the planet—in the oceans worldwide believed to contain marine plastic debris.
prefecture	In Japan, an administrative district about the size of a US county.
SDF (Japan Self-Defense Forces)	Japan's military forces.
seism	Earthquake.
Shibuya Station	Railway station in the Shibuya ward of Tokyo, Japan.
Shinto	A native religion of Japan.
Soka Gakkai	Worldwide Buddhist network that promotes peace, culture, and education through personal transformation and social contribution.
TEPCO (Tokyo Electric Power Company)	The largest electric power company in Japan; operator of the Fukushima Daiichi Nuclear Power Plant.

tsunami   Seismic sea wave; a long, high wave (or series of waves) created by an undersea earthquake, volcanic eruption, or other disturbance.

wa   Japanese term for harmony.

yen   Basic monetary unit of Japan.

CHRONOLOGY

2011 **March 11** A magnitude 9.0 undersea earthquake strikes off the northeast coast of Japan; a tsunami warning is issued. A tsunami wave hits the northeastern Japanese coast, causing massive damage and flooding; more than fifty aftershocks occur. External power is lost at the Fukushima Daiichi nuclear power plant and backup generators also go down; four of Japan's fifty-four nuclear plants are shut down. An evacuation order is issued for thousands of people living within one-and-a-half miles of the Fukushima Daiichi nuclear power plant; sixty to seventy thousand residents of the coastal city of Sendai are evacuated to shelters; the US Geological Service announces that the earthquake was the most powerful to hit Japan since records began.

March 12 Fires are reported in at least three prefectures; tsunamis continue to wash ashore on the northeast coast of Japan. Power is out in 4 million homes in Tokyo and surrounding areas; more than 1 million households have no water; more than 215,000 people are living in more than one thousand temporary shelters in five prefectures. Aid comes in from all over the world; a nuclear emergency is declared at the Fukushima Daiichi nuclear power plant, increasing fear of a nuclear meltdown. More earthquakes hit the west coast of Honshu; it is reported that radioactive substances could have leaked at Fukushima. Cooling systems have failed at three of the four units at Fukushima; electricity is out for at least 10 percent of Japan's homes. A hydrogen explosion occurs that blows away the upper part of a building housing a Fukushima Daiichi reactor; the earthquake is reported to have moved Japan's main island of Honshu by eight feet and shifted earth on its axis; at least 1,300 are dead and thousands more are missing.

March 13   Prime Minister Naoto Kan calls the March 11 disaster Japan's "most severe crisis" since the end of World War II. One hundred thousand Japan Self-Defense Forces personnel, 190 aircraft, and twenty-five ships are deployed to help with rescue efforts; rolling blackouts begin. US military forces stationed in Japan begin Operation Tomodachi to assist the relief effort; energy rationing is announced. The Japanese government reports that more than two hundred thousand people residing in the vicinity of the crippled nuclear reactors have been evacuated from the area.

March 14   A second explosion occurs at the Fukushima plant; prices fall on the Tokyo stock exchange.

March 15   An earthquake with a seismic intensity of 6 hits eastern Shizuoka Prefecture; a third explosion causes dangerous levels of radiation to leak from the Fukushima Daiichi plant.

March 16   The emperor of Japan addresses the nation via a video broadcast.

March 17   Foreign governments urge their citizens to leave Tokyo.

March 19   Abnormal levels of radiation are detected in milk and spinach near the Fukushima Daiichi nuclear plant.

March 23   The accident at the Fukushima Daiichi nuclear plant is upgraded from a Level 4 to a Level 5 on the International Nuclear Event Scale (INES); the Japanese government warns that radiation levels in the tap water in Tokyo and nearby towns are above levels safe for babies; milk and produce from the Fukushima region are banned.

March 25 | Japan's National Police Agency announces that more than ten thousand are dead.

April | The government officially designates the March 11 disaster the "Great East Japan Earthquake"; Tokyo Electric Power Company, which operates the Fukushima Daiichi nuclear plant, admits that radioactive water from the Fukushima reactor 2 is leaking into the ocean; the accident at the Fukushima Daiichi nuclear plant is upgraded to a Level 7, the highest level on INES.

May | More than one hundred thousand people may have lost their jobs as a result of the earthquake and tsunami; meltdowns are confirmed to have happened 60 hours and 101 hours after the earthquake at the Unit 3 and Unit 2 reactors of the Fukushima plant.

July | Kan calls for a nuclear-free Japan.

August | Kan announces his resignation.

2012 A reconstruction agency is formed to deal with rebuilding disaster-hit areas; an independent panel investigating the Fukushima nuclear disaster reports that the accident at the nuclear plant was "man-made"; the government announces that four of the reactors at Fukushima Daiichi are formally going to be "decommissioned"; Japan's last nuclear reactor shuts down; and Japan announces that it plans to abandon nuclear power by 2030 and will not begin construction on any nuclear reactors during that period.

2013   Japanese prime minister Shinzo Abe visits Miyagi
Prefecture and resolves to speed up reconstruction
efforts in disaster-hit areas; Japan's National Police
Agency count shows almost 16,000 dead and more than
2,500 missing as a result of the disaster.

FOR FURTHER READING

Books

Fred Bortz, *Meltdown!: The Nuclear Disaster in Japan and Our Energy Future*. Minneapolis, MN: Twenty-First Century Books, 2012.

Gretel Ehrlich, *Facing the Wave: A Journey in the Wake of the Tsunami*. New York: Pantheon Books, 2013.

Takumi Hayaska and Vukio Sasaki, *A Time of Disaster: The Great East Japan Earthquake and Tsunami*. Sendai City, Miyagi Prefecture, Japan: Sasaki Printing and Publishing, 2011.

Takashi Hirose, *Fukushima Meltdown: The World's First Earthquake-Tsunami-Nuclear Disaster*. CreateSpace Independent Publishing Platform, 2012.

Jeff Kingston, ed., *Natural Disaster and Nuclear Crisis in Japan: Response and Recovery After Japan's 3/11*. New York: Routledge, 2012.

Elmer Luke and David Karashima, eds., *March Was Made of Yam: Reflections on the Japanese Earthquake, Tsunami, and Nuclear Meltdown*. New York: Vintage, 2012.

Marcia Amidon Lusted, *The 2011 Japan Disasters*. Minneapolis, MN: ABDO Publishing, 2011.

David Pilling and Bill Emmott, *Tsunami: Japan's Post-Fukushima Future*. Washington, DC: Foreign Policy Magazine, 2011.

Cecile Pineda, *Devil's Tango: How I Learned the Fukushima Step by Step*. San Antonio, TX: Wings Press, 2012.

Richard J. Samuels, *3.11: Disaster and Change in Japan*. Ithaca, New York: Cornell University Press, 2013.

Patrick Sherriff, ed., *2:46: Aftershocks: Stories from the Japan Earthquake*. London: Enhanced Editions, 2011.

Itoko Suzuki and Yuko Kaneko, *Japan's Disaster Governance: How Was the 3.11 Crisis Managed?* New York: Springer, 2013.

Mark Willacy, *Fukushima: Japan's Tsunami and the Inside Story of the Nuclear Meltdowns.* South Yarra, Victoria, Australia: Macmillan Australia, 2013.

Periodicals

Hannah Beech, Lucy Birmingham, Tai Dirkse, and Krista Mahr, "How Japan Will Reawaken," *Time,* March 28, 2011.

Ken Belson and Norimitsu Onishi, "In Deference to Crisis, a New Obsession Sweeps Japan: Self-Restraint," *New York Times,* March 27, 2011.

Lucy Birmingham, "Japan's Earthquake Warning Systems Explained," *Time,* March 18, 2011.

Philip Brasor, "Scrutiny of Tohoku Reconstruction Funds Needed," *Japan Times,* September 23, 2012.

Geoff Brumfiel and Ichiko Fuyuno, "Japan's Nuclear Crisis: Fukushima's Legacy of Fear," *Nature,* March 7, 2012.

Lucille Craft, "Japan's Nuclear Refugees," *National Geographic,* December 2011.

Cody Crane and Karina Hamalainen, "The Disaster in Japan," *Science World,* May 9, 2011.

"The Death of Trust," *The Economist,* March 10, 2012.

Martin Fackler, "Civic Paralysis Seizes Tsunami-Stricken Town Still in Shambles," *New York Times,* September 12, 2011.

Pico Iyer, "Heroes of the Hot Zone," *Vanity Fair,* January 2012.

Eric Johnston, "Osaka Pushes Incendiary Tsunami Debris Plan," *Japan Times,* January 12, 2013.

David Jolly, Hiroko Tabuchi, and Keith Bradsher, "Tainted Water at 2 Reactors Increases Alarm for Japanese," *New York Times,* March 27, 2011.

Nicholas Köhler, "Life in No Man's Land," *Maclean's,* March 12, 2012.

Nancy Macdonald, Nicholas Köhler, Erica Alini, and Kate Lunau, "A Nation's Grief," *Maclean's,* March 28, 2011.

Fuyubi Nakamura, "Memory in the Debris: The 3/11 Great Japan Earthquake and Tsunami," *Anthropology Today,* June 2012.

Evan Osnos, "Aftershocks," *New Yorker,* March 28, 2011.

Evan Osnos, "The Fallout," *New Yorker,* October 17, 2011.

Tim Shorrock, "Naoto Kan and the End of 'Japan Inc.'," *The Nation,* April 4, 2011.

Jill Smolowe, Liz McNeil, Michiko Toyama, Kirk Spitzer, and Juliet Butler, "Disaster in Japan: Out of the Rubble," *People,* April 4, 2011.

Hiroko Tabuchi, "Tsunami Projections Offer Bleak Fate for Many Japanese Towns," *New York Times,* April 9, 2012.

Paul Theroux, "Nightmare and Defiance," *Newsweek,* March 28, 2011.

Patrick Tucker, "My First Meltdown: Lessons from Fukushima," *Futurist,* July/August 2011.

Neil Weinberg, "Dispatch from Tokyo: In Wake of Disaster, Japan Is at War," *Forbes,* March 14, 2011.

Sandra Sobieraj Westfall and Michiko Toyama, "After the Tsunami," *People,* March 26, 2012.

Alexandra Witze, "Making Waves," *Science News,* February 25, 2012.

Websites

Japan Disaster (www.guardian.co.uk/world/japan-earthquake-and-tsunami). This site offers comprehensive coverage from the time of the 2011 earthquake, tsunami, and nuclear disaster to the present by providing links to a broad range of *Guardian* articles, videos, interactive guides, photographs, and blogs dedicated to the triple disaster and its aftermath.

National Geographic Daily News (http://news.nationalgeographic.com/news/2011/03/pictures/110315-nuclear-reactor

-japan-tsunami-earthquake-world-photos-meltdown). This site offers photographs of the aftermath of the 2011 tsunami and the nuclear cleanup at Fukushima, as well as links to the tsunami and other disaster-related news, pictures, videos, and facts.

Opinion 3/11 (http://japanecho.net). This site provides what it titles "views from Japan on the March 11 disaster." Included are links to the March 16 message delivered by the emperor to the people of Japan; numerous high-quality photographs; 3/11 data on earthquakes, nuclear power, reconstruction, and the Tohoku region of Japan; and 3/11-related articles written by a broad range of individuals from diverse walks of life.

Slideshare.net (http://blog.slideshare.net/2011/03/22/news -scientific-analysis-and-photo-essays-of-japanese-disaster). This site provides links to news, scientific analysis, and photo essays of the March 11, 2011, disaster created and presented by people and groups from around the world. Each link is accompanied by a brief description of its content and its creators.

INDEX